AUSTRALIAN WOODTURNING PROJECTS

First published 2002 by
Interwood Holdings Pty Ltd
PO Box 4336
Loganholme DC,
Queensland
Australia 4129

Tel +617 3806 2288

Fax +617 3806 2277

Email: woodreview@ecn.net.au

Website: www.woodreview.com

Safety: Woodworking can be dangerous. do not undertake any work, process or action without adequate skill, training, safety equipment and/or awareness.

National Library of Australia Cataloguing-in-Publication entry:

Australian woodturning projects : the best of Australian wood review.

ISBN 0-9580551-0-6

1. Woodwork. I. Title : Australian wood review.

684.08

Publisher: Interwood Holdings Pty Ltd, Brisbane, Australia, 2002

Editors: Linda Nathan, Rafael Nathan

Layout: Rebecca Nathan, Linda Nathan

Digital imaging by Showads Omega Pty Ltd, Australia

Printed by PMP Print Pty Ltd, Australia

Australian Woodturning Projects

The Best of Australian Wood Review

30 of the Best Woodturning Projects from
Ten Years of Australian Wood Review

Published by Interwood Holdings Pty Ltd, Australia

Planet Sphere by Stephen Hughes

Woodturning as a craft and an art has undergone something of a renaissance in the USA, the UK, Europe and Australia. From early times it was a means of producing functional homewares as well as mechanical and architectural components. The onset of the industrial revolution and the development of electrically-driven lathes enhanced its potential for mass repetition. But in the latter half of the twentieth century not only have we seen a rise in popularity of this craft as part of a general revival in hand crafts, we have also seen the exponential evolution of woodturning as a means to creating unique and sculptural work.

Unlike techniques of joinery and furniture making, woodturning is a subtractive art—what has been taken away with chisels, gouges and scrapers cannot be put back. It's a fast way of transforming a medium and creating objects, however the skills needed to make turned curves come to life take a while to master. The authors of this collection of articles are sharing their collective experience with you, and the passion they have for their craft and their art is apparent in their personal and lively explanations.

The projects presented in this book were first printed in the quarterly magazine *Australian Wood Review*, now in its tenth year of publication. The magazine continues to publish stories written by some of Australia's leading furniture makers and woodturning exponents. From the diversity of items made and topics discussed here it is clear that the art of woodturning is a rich source of creative expression in Australia. The text of the stories presented has been revised and the visual presentation has been improved and in many cases totally altered to better present the information.

The publishers and editors of *Australian Wood Review* thank the authors for their contribution and hope you, the reader, will enjoy their writings and be able to build on their experience to develop your own skills and ideas.

Please note: Woodturning and woodworking can be dangerous, do not undertake any work, process or action without adequate skill, training, safety equipment and/or awareness. It is advisable to use a face shield to protect your face and eyes and to protect your respiratory system with dust collection equipment and personal dust protection shields and masks. Be aware of possible allergies to some timbers and the moulds present in spalted woods. Do not use machinery of any type when tired or under the influence of alcohol or drugs.

Contents

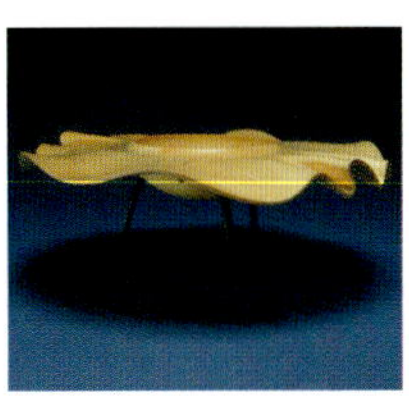

Contents

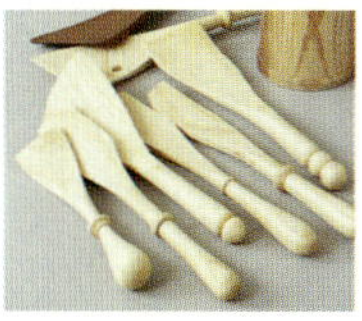

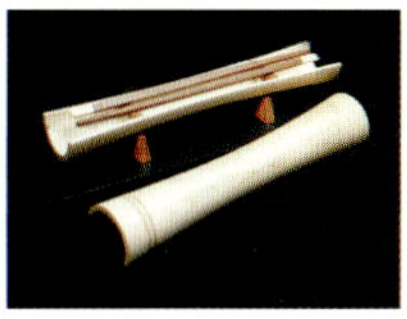

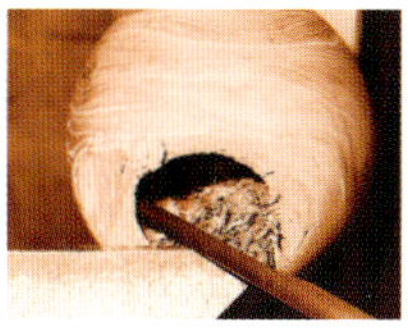

Turning Scent Flasks

Andrew Potocnik explores a variety of curves in his miniature scent flasks. Small turnings such as these, he writes, are perfect for using precious offcuts, while refining techniques and experimenting with form.

For some the act of creating objects is a way of exploring philosophical issues, for some it's a form of therapy or even escape, for others it's just a means to an income. Whatever your motivation, small-scale production runs can provide food for thought and even food for the table. Looking at works produced by other cultures and in other media may help to inspire forms you can turn. From primitive to medieval to modern times you will find forms which can be adapted to the finials, shoulders, steps and curves of the pieces you make. Where you put the belly of a curve will determine whether you create something which evokes a feeling of an Egyptian canopic jar, a classical arch, or an Islamic minaret.

The scent flasks shown provide numerous small-scale avenues of technical and aesthetic exploration. They are a perfect way to utilise offcuts of precious and even not-so-precious woods. I also find producing numerous copies of similar objects gives me the opportunity to refine my skills. I begin by rough turning timber between centres, and then transferring the blank to a scroll chuck. Using a chuck which generates plenty of grip with little fuss, leaves one end of the blank free to work on. Once mounted, I start rough turning the neck of the flask (photo 1) with a 10mm bowl gouge. I am often asked whether I have a selection of small tools set aside for making small objects such as these flasks. The answer is a simple no! Finely sharpened tools will perform most tasks, depending on your technique.

Next I use a diamond or spear-pointed scraper to create a depression (photo 2) into which I can insert a drill bit to hollow out the flask's interior. For this task I use a drill bit held in a Jacob's chuck, pushing it into the rotating blank as far as I feel is necessary (photo 3). Some turners may choose other methods of holding the drill bit.

Returning to the diamond-point scraper, I open out the neck of the flask, aiming for a smooth flowing line. Now the exterior of the neck has to be reworked to match the interior line. At this point I also pay attention to any detailing which may be applied to the area where the neck and body join. Steps, beads or V-cuts are only a few of the elements which may be considered at this stage. I like to create a definite break in form rather than simply running the neck directly into the body of the flask. This allows each individual component of the flask to stand out and be set off against its neighbouring component.

Keep in mind though, if you are using a highly figured timber, the form should not be too ornate, or it will create tension for the viewer, who won't know whether to look at the timber or the form. In this case it's better to concentrate on strength of form, rather than relying on too many details. Don't fall into the trap of relying on the timber itself to 'sell' your work.

Depending on your desired outcome, work the form down towards the foot. The flask I'm making here will stand

2

4

on a slender stem and foot, so it appears tall and graceful. Without the stem the form will tend to sit squat and have a heavier appearance. In this case a totally different set of aesthetics will be required to make these forms appear light and balanced.

On a technical point, don't forget that the closer you get to the chuck of your lathe, and the finer you turn the form, the less chance you have of going back and reworking portions already turned without causing the wood to chatter or tear. In the worst instance, you may even break off thin sections of wood.

Photo 4 shows the completed form sanded and turned right down to the foot. I sanded through to 320 grit and then oiled and waxed with a commercially prepared wax finish applied while the wood was still on the lathe. Once complete, the flask is ready to be separated from its stock base (photo 5). Here you can see how I support the flask with my left hand, which is in turn supported by my forearm resting against the headstock—this prevents the flask breaking off before the cut is complete.

For this flask I created a teardrop shape stopper, similar to those seen in contemporary Egyptian perfume bottles. I began by turning a tapered section to fit the opening flask. Once the overall diameter of this component is established, I sand it down until it fits perfectly (photo 6). Using a skew, I cut a line which will separate the teardrop form from the actual stopper.

The rest of the stopper is turned with a detail gouge. When you sand it, keep in mind the fragile nature of the thin portion of the wood which still joins the stopper to its stock. The finish is carefully applied at this stage. I use my left hand to support the stopper during this process and while cutting it free (photo 7).

When complete, place a couple of drops of essential oil into the flask and wait for it to permeate through the wood. Alternatively, you may choose to simply add the flask to your collection of turnings made from cherished pieces of wood.

A Hollow Form

The key to turning hollow forms with 'soul', writes Stephen Hughes, is good design and technical expertise.

It's not uncommon to see a turning which, despite an excellence of execution and brilliance of finish, somehow lacks something. The importance of good design, that is, having regard for harmony of form and line, is something that can never be overlooked.

The most important view of the closed shape bowl is the profile, and that holds the key to that form coming alive, having if you like, a soul. Without a balanced shape the profile is lost and the strength of the bowl will rest on its surface appearance, rather than any design element. The dynamic flow of the turned surface will be a combination of its two dimensional profile and its three dimensional form as viewed from various angles.

The good news is that developing an eye for balanced, pleasing forms is possible. An excellent starting point is to develop your ability to visualise forms by sketching, drawing and even tracing them. I often start with the dimensions of the blank I am using and sketch this on paper as a rectangular form. This defines the outer perimeters of the piece. Within this frame I begin to sketch the profile shapes I want to achieve in my turning.

Some forms have universal appeal and they all seem to rely on visually pleasing curves and balanced proportions of height to width. Look around you for ideas, especially at the works of other artists who have worked in wood, metal, glass, ceramic and even plastic. The 'right' shape is the one which is most visually pleasing.

A finished form must not only look balanced, it must be a joy to hold and feel. To achieve this, the exterior profile must be matched by the interior. For the hollowed form to feel right, avoid heavy or thick bases and strive for thin, even wall thickness.

Production Steps

1. Select a suitable piece of stock that will enable you to achieve the dimensions of form you desire. Remember that the selection you make will affect how close you can stay to your original idea. Note any natural flaws and decide whether to leave or remove them.

2. For this project I chose a coolibah burl—these are wonderfully tight burls, typically with a swirling marble-like pattern with reddish browns and pinks that are often mixed with the pale surrounding sapwood. The burl was 220mm diameter x 145mm high.

3. Cut your stock into a turning blank. To cut a rounded blank from this rough surfaced burl, I used a circular template which I nailed lightly into the top surface of the piece. In this way I kept the chainsawn flat surface securely on the bandsaw table as I cut the blank (photo 1).

4. Mount your blank on the lathe. I drilled a hole into the natural rough surface of the burl for mounting on a large screw thread held in a scroll chuck and used my tailstock for added support. You may choose to use a faceplate on another combination.

At this stage, besides having a safe and secure holding method, you need to consider which end will be the top or bottom of the bowl. Plan the latter so that loss of stock will be minimal and any damage caused by holding methods (such as screw holes) can be removed.

5. Remove excess material from the base area of the bowl and form a step for rechucking the piece for hollowing (photo 2). I used a deep fluted gouge for the roughing work as this works quickly and leaves clean surface cuts. The stepped base area is cut with a spindle gouge shaped to a lady finger tip profile. This step can be scraped with a square-nose scraper if you find this more accurate.

6. Before rechucking, the top profile is refined and some deep holes left by some hungry borers (who were still dining), were cut away (photo 3). The tailstock was then removed and the detail inside the stepped foot turned. The bowl will have a curved base with fine turned beads for base detail.

7. Next, I rechucked the base into a *Vicmarc* 4-jaw universal scroll chuck, but any good quality chucking system could be used (photo 4).

8. The top profile of the form is further refined. Because of the unsightly borer tracks I decided to remove the natural rim (photo 5). Note that the opening of this form is between a third and a half the diameter of the whole piece. In this case the size of the opening (approximately 75mm) allows for easy hollowing and smoothing of the interior surface. A smaller opening would have made both operations much more difficult.

9. I have turned a rim that will have a small bead around the opening. The main shaping cuts were achieved with the deep fluted bowl gouge and details around the beaded rim were cut with a spindle gouge. The detail of a bead should be crisp and well defined to enhance the line of the opening.

10. Use a deep fluted gouge to rough out the internal form, concentrating on the central area of bowl (photo 6). By boring an entry hole into the piece with a drill bit you can quickly gain a depth guide for your bowl. I use a 25mm 0Forstner bit held in a Jacob's chuck in the tailstock and leave around 15mm wall thickness in the base. Check the material in the foot area if you have turned this detail.

2

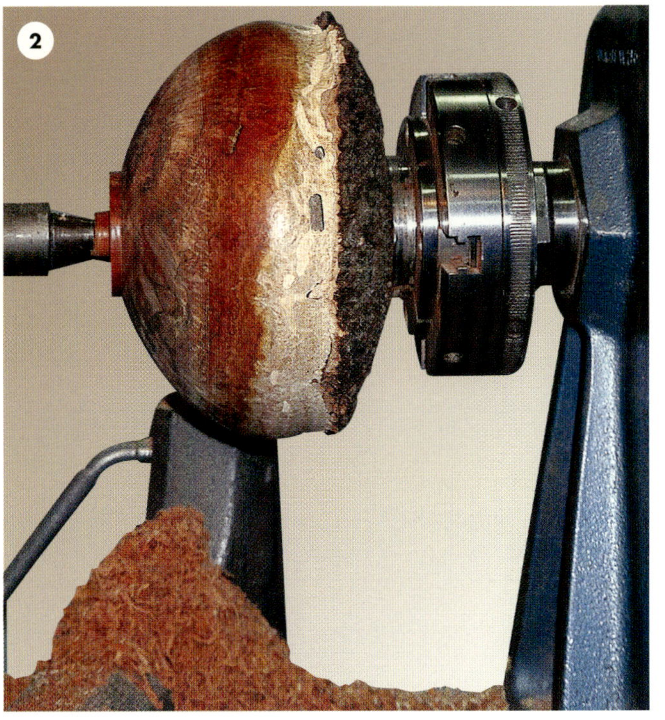

3

4

11. Continue roughing as much material from under the opening as possible leaving the walls about 15mm thick in the lower area of the bowl for support.

12. To thin down the wall thickness (to about 2mm) I start at the top using a 12mm x 8mm round-

nose scraper. This allows me to come in from the opposite side of the opening to undercut the rim and still obtain an internal curve that gives me an even wall thickness. Note the negative rake on the tool as the cutting edge is pointed below the level of the tool rest to prevent catching (photo 7).

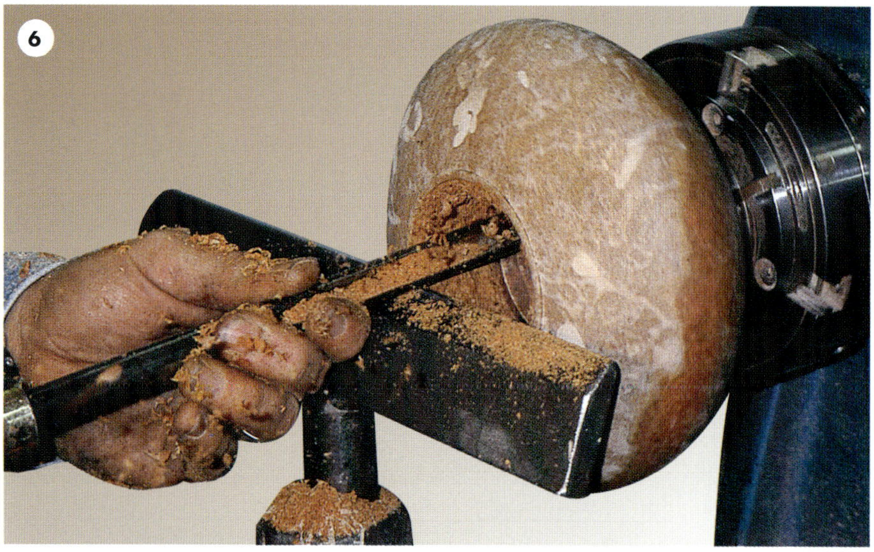

13. In photo 8, I am using a *DAHT* to hollow the form, however other systems can be used.

14. Finish the inside surface and the top to middle outer surface and apply your chosen finish (I used Danish oil). I usually make the opening wide enough to be able to hand sand the interior surface. If you can't reach inside you will have to make up abrasive pads on dowels to get inside; this can be a time consuming process. I start at 80 grit and progress through 120, 180, 240, 320, 400, to 600 grit. It's worth noting that most internationally recognised hollow turners (such as David Ellsworth and Bill Hunter) achieve extremely even tool cuts on the inside of their forms which they leave as natural turned surfaces. You only have to hold one of their pieces to appreciate their mastery of hollowing techniques. This sort of skill takes a lot of time to learn.

8

15. Finally, to finish the base the piece is removed from the chuck and re-mounted onto a jam fit chuck, which needs to be a very accurate fit. The expanding jaws of a universal chuck or similar on a thin wall can exert enough pressure to crack them, so remember to be careful. Using a cushion block (a small dowel with a leather face), bring the tailstock centre up onto the base. Remove any excess foot and refine the base before sanding and polishing again.

16. The piece is then signed and re-oiled. Oiling the piece again a couple of times at weekly intervals will ensure a natural lustre.

No matter how well you have designed your initially planned form, nature will have the final say. In this case I had to refine the form and modify it around a natural flaw which another turner may have decided to make a feature of. Above all though, the key to giving your hollow forms 'soul' is to obtain the profile you have visualized, and then bring it to life by achieving even, thin walls.

Extra Tips on Hollow Turning

1. Make sure you have the tools capable of safely achieving the job. If your top opening allows it, use a strong and heavy tool rest. I use a 300mm section of 35 x 12mm steel welded onto a solid rod that fits my tool rest support.

2. If your turning has a small opening (less than 30mm), use scraping techniques which create chips and dust to allow for ease of cleaning out (a compressor helps to blow out trapped waste). A nozzle attached to a vacuum cleaner can be helpful.

3. Keep checking the wall thickness with an accurate set of figure-eight calipers or similar. Be patient, hollowing is a demanding technique. A neat trick is to leave the wall thickness approximately 10mm (get it even of course) and then thin the wall from the outside to 2-3mm.

Turning a Bowl

The basics of bowl turning and tool handling by Richard Raffan.

This project shows you how to make a simple, well balanced, open bowl from a solid blank using standard tools and chucks. This form allows you to become familiar with all the basic cuts, and as work proceeds you can see what you're doing at all times with minimal risk of the edge catching.

Bowls are made in two stages: first you turn and finish the outside, gripping the blank by what will be the top of the bowl. Then the part-turned form is re-chucked and gripped by the foot for hollowing. And you'll also see how to re-chuck a bowl so you can clean up or alter the foot.

Tools and Wood Required

You need four tools: a deep fluted 1/2" bowl gouge with rounded wings, a shallow 1/2" or 9/16" gouge with a fingernail grind, a 1-1/4" heavy, slightly

A General Approach to Tool Handling

The key to fine turning is to avoid forcing the tool into or against the wood. Let the wood come to the tool, let the lathe do the work.You need to hold the tool so that in the event of a catch your body can absorb the impact. Have your power ready to counteract the leverage, not constantly expended, forcing the tool into the wood. Keep your lower hand on the handle near the ferrule with the handle under your forearm, so the tool is like an extension of your arm. Try to keep the handle into your side, and move with the tool so your weight is behind it.

Efficient removal of the wood occurs when a sharp edge slices the wood rather than rips or scrapes it. In general, the portion of the edge cutting slices best when presented at about 45° to the oncoming wood and this applies to all tools. The easiest way to cut curves is to use a gouge held near horizontal and pointing in the direction you're cutting with the bevel rubbing the wood.

This will give you plenty of control over the edge because the bevel shoulder acts as a secondary fulcrum from which you can pivot the edge. The moment the edge starts cutting there should be a smooth surface against which the bevel can rub, and it is on this that the next portion of the cut is based.

Any blemish on this surface will be reflected in the course of the cutting edge, so if you get chatter marks you need to go back to a smooth section of the curve, usually near the base and start again, riding through the bumps and across the dips.

radiused scraper, and a depth drill (made by inserting a twist drill into a handle).

My self-centering 4-jaw scroll chucks are fitted with step jaws; I don't know how serious bowl turners manage without these wonderful accessories. Most chucks will adapt to a centre screw chuck, but a dedicated screw centre is better and will reduce your frustration levels by freeing up your chuck for measuring and other jobs.

Your early bowl blanks should be about 200mm (8") diameter and 75mm (3") thick, bandsawn from any seasoned wood which is easy to work. Here I use forest sheoak. You will find air-dried material easier to work and less dusty than kiln-dried. If you have only unseasoned timber you'll need to rough turn your bowl then set it aside for a few months to season and warp, before re-chucking it to complete the job.

Note: A face shield should always be worn when turning bowls.

Roughing the Outside

Before mounting the wood on the lathe, check the lathe speed, erring on the side of caution. Spin a 200mm (8") x 75mm (3") blank at between 800-1100 rpm at first and up to 1500rpm once it's running true. If the lathe vibrates, lower the speed. This can be tedious unless you have a variable speed control, but the time taken can save you a nasty accident.

Mount the blank on the lathe by what will be the top of the bowl. A screw

5

6

7

chuck is the quickest and easiest way to hold the wood on the lathe (photo 1). If you are using the screw provided with one of the standard chucks, increase the support area of the chuck using a plywood or MDF washer, otherwise use a faceplate with screws. You can further secure the blank by using the tail centre support.

A round blank of even density should be well balanced as it spins on the lathe, so I rarely true up a disk before turning the profile. Set the rest at an angle across the corner of the blank and use a gouge rolled over to about 45° with the bevel facing the wood and the handle dropped about 15-20° below horizontal (photo 2). This is a shear cut, but because the bevel doesn't always rub there is little fine control of the edge and the surface tends to be ridged. The idea now is to sweep the edge through a series of arcs into the wood to get the bulk off as quickly as possible.

Have your left hand planted firmly on the rest to act as a fulcrum against which the tool can pivot as you start the cut, pushing the handle towards centre. Move the handle with your body rather than your hand: you'll get more power and control with less effort. Once the edge is cutting, start to squeeze the tool left along the rest with your left hand. By squeezing with the left hand as the edge pivots left you take a broad sweeping cut, and you can adjust the thickness of the shaving by rolling the tool slightly clockwise with your right hand. Don't force the edge into the wood: just let the wood come to the tool and the lathe do the work.

At this stage you'll need to move the rest often. You should stop the lathe and swing the wood by hand to check that it spins clear of the repositioned rest before restarting the lathe. I don't worry too much about the quality of cut at this stage; the idea is to rough the form out as quickly as possible, then turn the foot before finishing the curve of the profile.

The Base And The Foot

If you have a chuck with step jaws, you can turn a foot to fit. The jaws shouldn't leave a mark if the foot is slightly smaller than the true circle of the jaws. For the bowl to sit flat, the base must be concave, and I like to add a few beads or grooves for decoration as well.

It's easy to remove more wood than necessary as you true the base, so have the tool on its side as for the roughing cuts, but this time only squeeze the edge into the rim of the uneven base (photo 3). Don't push the handle away from you, rather the tool should be as if hinged at your hip, held solid against your body while the edge is squeezed into the wood until the tic-tic-tic noise of the cut goes, indicating a trued surface. If the blank is very uneven take a series of little squeezing cuts from the rim into centre to true the base. With the rim trued, roll the tool 180° for a shear cut from the rim into the centre (photo 4).

Mark the diameter of the foot (photo 5) and cut to the line using the nose of a shallow gouge for a series of small cuts (photo 6). Keep the bevel parallel to the lathe axis. A fingernail ground shallow gouge lets you get into corners better than a deep fluted gouge. Start the cut with the gouge on its side with the bevel aligned in the direction you're cutting and the flute facing outwards. The handle should be dropped 35°-45° below horizontal with your left hand keeping the tool pinned firmly to the rest. Bring the edge through an arc into the wood by raising the handle. If the gouge isn't right on its side a catch is near certain as the wood bears down on the unsupported upper side of the edge.

Refine the base using a heavy slightly radiused skewed scraper (photo 7). Aim to sweep the edge across the surface, gently stroking it using no more than 5mm (1/4") of the edge at one time. You can create a recessed dome by easing the left corner into the wood.

Completing The Profile

Make the final shearing cuts on the profile, working from the smaller to larger diameter. Here the shallow gouge is rolled on its side (photo 8). If you get chatter marks or ridges, either you're pushing the tool too hard against the

8

9

10

wood, or you don't have the bevel rubbing. Start the cut again near the foot and hold the tool more firmly cutting through the bumps and across the dips.

Clearly you will have difficulty in starting a shear cut right at the top of the foot, so you need to take a very delicate shear cut against the grain using the long nose of the shallow gouge as in photo 9, or use a scraper. A good shear cut should leave the surface ready for sanding, but you're not always that lucky. Any patches of slightly torn grain difficult to remove with abrasives can mostly be eliminated by shear scraping.

Shear scraping involves stroking the wood very gently with an edge rolled to around 45° to the wood (photo 10). Tilt the tool on its side and drag it gently along the rest using the lower half of the edge. I like a small burr from a 60 grit grinding wheel for most situations, but harder woods or particularly recalcitrant grain needs a honed edge. Shavings should be minuscule and curly, or dust.

Sanding And Finishing The Profile

With the turning completed you can sand and finish the outside. I generally hand sand a profile unless particularly difficult grain demands power sanding. I prefer abrasives with a light flexible cloth backing which is more expensive than paper-backed abrasive, but it lasts way longer and generally cuts better. Work through the grits from 100 to 150, 220, 360 and finer if you feel so inclined.

With the sanding completed I stop the lathe and slop oil liberally over the surface. Then I hold a block of soft beeswax against the spinning wood to build up a thin layer of wax which is then melted into the wood by applying a soft cloth. For utilitarian bowls use a vegetable (cooking) oil or a proprietary salad bowl finish.

Hollowing The Bowl

The bowl is gripped by the foot for hollowing (photo 11). My strategy is to drill a depth hole, then use a gouge as far as I can with the bevel rubbing, finally completing the curve across the bottom with a scraper. Begin the hollowing process by truing the face, then drill a depth hole. The depth hole does two things. First it establishes the depth to which you will hollow, saving constant stops to measure. Secondly, you remove the centre of the blank which is difficult to turn and the source of many catches.

A depth drill is easy to make by inserting a standard 6mm (1/4") or 9mm (3/8") twist drill 150mm-200mm (6"-8") long into a handle. I grind marks up the length of the drill to help me gauge a depth, or you can use an elastic band. The hole from the screw centre should be at centre, so all you do is mark the depth required on the drill and push it into the hole. If you keep the drill parallel to the lathe axis it should go in easily. The end gets very hot very quickly so watch out for your fingers as the tool and shavings come out.

Now you can get on with the hollowing using a deep fluted gouge. Work back from centre directing the cuts as much as possible towards the chuck (photo 12). The hazard here is the

it easier using a wide tool than one narrower. Although the scraper is 32mm (1-1/4") wide, I use only a small portion of the edge at one time. This is not a moulding tool: you can use all of the edge at sometime, but not all at once. Keep the tool flat on the rest and sweep the edge through a broad arc to keep the curve flowing. Don't even think of scraping up the side towards the rim because the thin wall will flex, the edge will catch and the bowl most likely blow apart.

tool kicking back as you start the cut. Catches occur when the pressure of the wood bears on an unsupported edge, so if you start with the gouge flat and flute up it will catch every time. Start every cut with the gouge on its side and the flute facing centre (photo 13). Begin with the handle dropped below centre 30°-45° so you can raise the handle to bring the edge through an arc into the wood. Once the tool is in the wood, keep the bevel rubbing and rotate the tool very slightly anti-clockwise to get a fatter shaving.

When you come to the final shear cuts the bowl wall is somewhat flexible. If you push too hard you'll have chatter marks unless you have your hand on the outside of the bowl to equalize the pressure of the cut. On the final cut I go as far round the curve as possible with the bevel rubbing, then use a scraper across the bottom which I find gives me greater control of the form.

It is possible to shear cut right to the bottom of the bowl with a gouge, but I prefer the control achieved using a wide scraper with a flattish curve which is slightly tighter than the curve I want to cut (photo 14). Heavy cuts can be made sweeping the tool across the surface toward the base. Finishing cuts should barely stroke the surface.

When cutting a broad curve you'll find

Sanding The Inside

I prefer to power sand the inside of a bowl using cloth-backed self adhesive discs mounted in an angle drill (photo 15). In part this is for speed, but it also helps maintain the sweep of the internal curve, especially across the bottom and at centre. Bumps and dips can easily develop when hand sanding. A standard drill also does the job, but it is more difficult to control and always requires two hands.

If you are hand sanding and a bump develops across the centre, stop the lathe and rotate it slowly by hand, sanding across the centre using a soft sanding pad to back the abrasive. A piece of foam rubber or rolled up cloth is ideal. This ensures that the very centre gets as much attention as the rest of the inside. Once the sanding is completed, apply an oil and wax finish.

If you are using step jaws or expanding standard jaws within a recess, the bowl will now be finished. However the bowl will often look better without a foot or feel better with the base turned thinner. In either case you need to remount the bowl gripping it by the rim.

Refining the Foot

Most manufacturers offer large bowl jaws as an accessory which enable you to grip a bowl by the rim, but an inexpensive option is to make your own jam chuck from an MDF or timber off-cut (photo 16). Here the bowl is jammed into a chuck. The tail-centre is used for security, with an MDF scrap protecting the bowl from the centre cone. The foot is removed by taking very light shear-scraping cuts using a shallow gouge on its side.

Wood is a wonderful knock-about material. A bowl like this, used with care, will survive us all and look better for use. And remember that whilst the first dent or stain of daily use is a minor disaster, a thousand make a patina.

Figure of Blackwood

After careful consideration of the unique properties of his medium, Vaughn Richmond creates a hollow turning with a carved decoration.

1

Australia has some of the world's best turning timbers. As a Western Australian woodturner, I served my apprenticeship on tough, hard WA desert woods like gidgee, mallee and sandalwood, and the eucalypts from the south-west forest areas around Pemberton. Blackwood (*Acacia melanoxylon*) grows mainly in Victoria and Tasmania and is recognised as a high quality ornamental timber. The tree belongs to the wattle family, and is a hardwood. It has been carved, turned and made into furniture since the early nineteenth century.

When I got this piece of timber the first thing I did was to take a shaving off and smell the real wood! The colour and grain showed potential, however it was the beautiful figure which really needed to be 'exploited'. This piece of blackwood reminded me of beautiful fiddleback woods such as American mahogany, highly prized by talented musical instrument makers who delight in making an instrument to suit the wood, rather than finding the wood to make an instrument!

The design phase took ages, with the important task of assessing the grain and trying to imagine which side would be a better top or bottom, and how best to show off the figure. I believe the surface of highly figured and beautifully grained timber should be left reasonably natural, free from garish colours, knobbly additions or excessive enhancements. This makes the shape even more critical, as each work needs a special 'lift' to highlight the wonderful artistry of nature.

I planned to turn a hollow form without a foot or base, so as not to restrict the natural flow of the grain, and with just a small amount of carving on the top. After deciding which part was to be the top, the work was hot glued to a scrap 'false' faceplate, and the base roughed out (photo 1). At this stage the lathe speed was kept fairly slow due to the imbalance in the blank. This was an opportunity to test my cutting angles and turning techniques on the blackwood. Thankfully, I found

2

3

its turning characteristics were similar to some of the local eucalypts, except the blackwood was prone to chipping if the cutting angle wasn't quite right. This was corrected by slightly altering the cutting angle of my 3/8" bowl gouge, and rubbing the bevel quite hard during the cutting process.

Turning the base down to the required shape was a relatively easy task, although it is important to consider that the shape of the bottom needs to be in proportion with where you think the top might start (photo 2)! This is where you need to stop the lathe from time to time and inspect the work to get it clear in your mind where the edges are supposed to be, double checking the shape is what you want.

Once the shape is deemed to be correct, and all the bumpy bits turned down correctly, the next step is to sand and seal the work. The form was sanded down to 800 grit paper and a liberal application of sealer applied. The sealer protects the wood from dirty fingers and greasy marks, and secondly (the best bit), allows you to see the real beauty of the pattern and grain for the first time!

This work does not have a foot, so the trick here is to contour the shape of the base with a profile gauge (photo 3) and turn the 'false' faceplate to match (photo 4). Next, hot glue the work to the faceplate using a ribbon of glue on the contact area of the faceplate.

There are several methods you can use to centralise the work—here are two ways. Prior to hot gluing the work to the faceplate, you can conduct a dry run, and adjust the work so the tail centre holds the work in balance. Keep rotating and adjusting the work by hand until the bowl is in the centre (trial and error), mark the 'best' tail centre indent, then apply the hot glue. You can also use a centre finder or compass to locate the centre of the work, but once again, do a dry run by placing the work on the faceplate and bringing the tail centre up to it. Rotate the work slowly by hand and check if any readjustment is needed to centralise it. Apply a ribbon of hot glue on the contact area of the faceplate and use the tail centre to hold the work against the faceplate while the glue sets (photo 5).

The use of a suitable saw-tooth bit can help get the hollowing started. It is important to measure and mark the bit, so that the depth of the drilling is controlled. In photo 6 the tape on the shank of the bit shows the depth. After the hole is drilled, I usually tape the top of the work, as the stresses of hollow turning can sometimes split the top, especially if you are turning a thin walled vessel.

With the hollowing complete (photo 7), it was time to remove the tape and start scribbling the design for the carving on the work. This is always the hard part, as the enhancement needs to be in concert with the shape and the grain of the timber. It is easy to get carried away with cutting, carving and colouring the timber, to the point where the ornamentation dominates the work.

As a general rule, if the timber is plain and dull a suitable amount of ornamentation will make the work pleasing to the eye. If the timber exhibits beautiful natural colour, grain or figure, then perhaps the enhancement should be kept to a minimum.

After many hours of scribbling and rubbing out with 320 grit paper, I decided on a small amount of carving from the centre to the rim (photo 8), which produced a nice overlapping effect. This was finished off with an inlay of Irish bog oak to complement the honey-coloured blackwood, along with some gold wire inserts to set off the colour of the dark coloured oak.

To finish this work, eight fine coats of satin/matt lacquer were sprayed on, and then rubbed right back to the surface. The oak inlay was glued into the recess prior to the last coat, and the final sanding was done with 800 grit wet and dry paper. Blackwood is a really nice timber to turn provided you keep your tools very sharp. A piece of timber like this one, which had exceptional figure and grain, deserves special attention for the potential it holds.

7

8

A Winged Vessel

With this 'winged' vessel, Terry Martin thinks laterally and adds value to his work by utilising more of the timber he starts out with.

Often the only way to obtain good quality timber is in long lengths sawn for cabinet making or other straight line work. If you want to use it for turning, there is an inevitable waste of timber as the corners are cut off on the bandsaw, or the shavings pile up under your lathe.

You can often charge more for larger woodturnings, as people like to feel they are getting a lot for their dollar. I used to be very frustrated when I obtained a piece of timber, say 300mm square. The diagonal measurement, from corner to corner, was around 430mm and I wanted to utilise that extra wood instead of mulching my garden with the waste.

Square-rimmed vessels were pioneered by Vic Wood long ago and have been much imitated, so I wanted a new idea. The result is my winged vessels, which are larger than simple circular cutting allows.

This project starts with a piece of Huon pine 200mm square and 100mm thick. Draw diagonal lines from corner to corner on one face to find the exact centre, drill a hole and mount the blank on a screw chuck. It's possible to use a small faceplate, but for this size I find a quality screw chuck secure enough.

Truing up the base.

Marking the spigot diameter.

Cutting away from the base.

Cutting inward from the corners.

The finished base.

The imaginary line.

Safety First

There are a few important rules for turning out of round pieces:

1. The speed selected should be as fast as you can go without vibration. Cutting will be intermittent when the corners are passing the tool. A faster speed means that cutting will be more continuous—ie: 'cutcutcutcut' not 'cut...cut...cut...cut'.

2. Position the toolrest as close to the work as you can. It is important to always rotate the work 360° by hand to be sure that no part of the work contacts the toolrest (this applies no matter what you are turning).

3. When cutting you should draw an imaginary line parallel with the toolrest and extending far longer than its length. No part of your hand or body should cross that line. As long as all of you is on the opposite side of the toolrest to all of the work, you'll be safe. Just keep that invisible line in your mind and remember that the spinning corners of the work will be invisible. A flexible lamp is very useful here as it can be angled across the work to give a solid view of the spinning corners.

Method

1. True the base of the blank, concentrating on the centre where the spigot will be cut (photo 1). It is not yet necessary to cut the corners. Next, mark the diameter of the spigot. As I am going to remount this piece in a scroll chuck, I only need a small spigot. To give the best grip and avoid uneven crushing of the spigot (which can cause it to snap off) make sure the chuck is set so the jaws are circular. On most scroll chucks this position is found with the jaws slightly open. I use a pair of dividers to transfer this diameter to the base of the blank, making sure that only the left hand leg of the dividers is in contact with the wood and on the rest, ensuring there is no catch (photo 2).

2. After shaping the spigot, cut away from the base as if starting an ordinary bowl. Stop at the point where cutting begins to be intermittent (photo 3). Then cut inwards towards the centre of the piece leaving the tips of the corners intact so the curve blends

The marked opening and rim.

Top and bottom curves blended.

The shaded areas to be cut.

Shaded areas visible as the work spins.

Cutting with the parting tool.

Sighting over the top to refine the curve.

in with the first outward cuts (photo 4).

The reason for cutting in this direction is that an outward cut may pull the corners off the piece. During this intermittent cutting it is important to maintain downward pressure on the tool rest so the gouge does not jump around as it contacts the work. In this kind of cutting the old rule of keep the bevel rubbing is not only inapplicable, it is actually impossible. The aim of the last stage is clearer in photo 5, which shows the finished cut. The two curves have blended into each other and there is an impression of a bowl embedded in a block of wood.

3. Next, turn over the piece and mount it in the chuck. If you are worried that the spigot is not strong enough, you can run a line of *Superglue* around the base of the spigot and let it harden before you fit it in the chuck. The glue will penetrate along the grain and make the spigot rock-hard. It may help to draw a line on the outside of the block to illustrate the imaginary vessel you are shaping (photo 6). Although you will not actually cut most of this curve, you need to blend the top and bottom of the vessel into its line.

4. The size of the vessel opening is decided in this case by the 100mm sawtooth bit I am going to use to start hollowing. Having marked the opening, cut a flat rim around it (photo 7). Then cut the rest of the top in the same way as the bottom, again ending up with a balanced curve (photo 8). The balance of top and bottom is clear and the imbedded vessel is starting to take shape.

5. Next, draw shaded areas on the square edge of the blank

Cutting with the Stewart tool.

to indicate where the wings will be cut (photo 9). If the light is positioned correctly, the shading will appear to be continuously in view while the piece spins. It will then be easy to accurately make the cuts (photo 10). The tailstock can be brought up for extra security at this stage. Again taking care that the toolrest clears the work, I use a parting tool in a horizontal position to plunge cut into the spinning corners and remove the shaded areas (photo 11).

If you are not confident using a parting tool at this point, you may feel more secure using a longer, heavier tool such as a *Stewart System Slicer* (photo 13). After the grooves are cut to the point where the tool is cutting continuously, sight over the top of the spinning work and blend the curve into the imaginary line that runs from the base to the top (photo 12).

Because I am going to texture the surface of most the of vessel, I am not worried about a fine finish. Part of the reason is that it would be practically impossible to sand the out-of-round portions of the work.

The wings and diameter marked out.

6. When the shape is satisfactory, mark a circle on the top at the widest diameter of the vessel, then mark the wings (photo 14). You have the option of leaving four wings, but I find that two are less busy to the eye and give a pleasing curve.

7. Next, cut away the unwanted parts of the rim on the bandsaw (photo 15). To refine the curve of the vessel wall where I have cut away the rim, I hold the vessel and sand freehand against a belt sander.

8. When the outside has been shaped, the vessel is remounted in the chuck to leave hands free for the next operation. At this stage a *Black & Decker Powerfile*, or similar small, hand-held belt sander can be used to further refine the outside wall.

I start hollowing with the 100mm saw-tooth bit, which removes a massive amount of wood very quickly. Then I finish hollowing with the *Stewart System* hooker. After hollowing is complete I sand the interior and rim to give a smooth contrast to the textured surface of the rest of the vessel. I can then either reverse-mount the vessel and turn off the spigot, of plane it off and sand the foot.

There is no reason why the hollowing can't be done at an earlier stage before the bandsawing so the piece doesn't need to be remounted. I simply find it easier to use calipers to check the wall thickness with most of the rims removed.

I usually use a *Foredom Woodcarver* with a tungsten bit to refine the wing shapes (photo 16). There are other systems that will do the same job, or if you don't want to buy a powered rotary cutter it is possible to buy a flexible drive shaft that can be driven from your lathe with a Jacob's chuck. If you are a glutton for punishment you can do the whole job with rasps and sandpaper.

9. After I am happy with the shape I use a small ball-shaped cutter to texture the surface. This is done by repeated taps with the bit on the surface until the whole is stippled to a uniform texture. It is important to cut with the grain or a furred surface will result.

Cutting the excess away on the bandsaw.

Shaping with the Foredom carver.

10. The final surface can be lightly buffed using a nylon rotary brush or a cloth buffer mounted in the lathe. This will remove any leftover furry bits. I prefer a wipe-on, wipe-off *Penetrol* finish as the textured surface doesn't work with all materials. A spray finish would also work well.

The result is an exotic winged vessel and the extra work has added value while saving timber. I encourage you to look at your turning blanks and think before you cut off any supposed excess. Maybe you can add a lot more value with some lateral thinking and extra work.

Turning Hollow Miniatures

Less can be more when simple, homemade tools are used to turn smaller, often discarded sections of wood. Andrew Potocnik shows how.

The spectacular timbers and the vast range of tools and techniques which well known turners use has always been a constant cause of awe amongst more amateur exponents. However, with a little know-how and only minimal tools, even the greenest turner can create striking pieces.

During a visit to New Zealand, I was privileged to examine the work of several turners, in particular the miniature hollow forms of David Ellsworth. I was enthralled by the tactile qualities of these pieces, mesmerised by their weight, smooth lines, and, most of all, their size. Enclosing a full form in the clasp of one hand is a tactile joy rarely experienced, especially one turned to perfection by a master such as Ellsworth. I was hooked! And, being something of a wood-miser, the thought of maximising smaller, virtually useless pieces of timber really appealed to me. I was

instantly inspired to try converting discards into new pieces.

The Making

There are a couple of ways of gripping timber for turnings of this type. Larger pieces may be gripped directly in a chuck. I find a scroll chuck most practical because of its holding strength and simple operation. Small limb sections may need to be fixed to a scrap carrier. For this I use a cyanoacrylate glue (such as *Superglue* or *Loctite*), which bonds almost instantly to wet materials. For peace of mind I allow plenty of time for the glue to dry—overnight is ideal as blanks can be glued and clamped on the lathe before packing up for the night.

When turning on this scale, you can use complete limb sections, incorporating heart and sapwood, from a small piece of timber otherwise considered useless. However, further potential exists, depending on the alignment of timber. For example, prominent vertical grain will produce vertical rings around a bulbous form, while contrasting sapwood can form the neck of a vessel while the body is made up of heartwood. In this case I selected a small section of West Australian Goldfields native willow, *Pittosporum phylliraeoides*.

Photo 1 shows use of a thin-walled detail gouge to shear scrape the vessel form, refining it from its rough turned beginnings. Retaining bark on the neck portion created a visual connection between the tree form and the turned vessel. Don't make the base too small at this point, as it could break once pressure resulting from hollowing is applied. When working on such a small scale, it's important to ensure the form is balanced and in proportion—imperfections are more obvious in miniatures than they are on larger pieces. For any piece to appeal to the discerning eye, form must be spot-on. Poor line or incorrect balance can ruin several hours of intense work.

Once I'm happy with the form, I sand lightly only with 180 grit abrasive before hollowing, leaving the final sanding for later, so drying out of the wood is lessened. Photo 2 shows the sanded form held in a scroll chuck. Note the base is left fairly large to provide plenty of support for hollowing.

Hollowing is basically a 'blind' process when working on this scale. Several tools created from Allen keys and hardened concrete nails are all I use. A little bending and grinding quickly creates a set of miniature tools suited to scaled-down hollow turning. A concrete nail ground to a round-nose forms the scraper, which is my main hollowing tool. With a shaft of about 70mm in length, it easily removes waste material. Unfortunately though, waste accumulates quickly inside the vessel, so it's necessary to empty shavings frequently. A piece of stiff wire bent to a right angle at one end performs this task

A selection of homemade tools for small-scale work, left to right: a cleaning hook, two concrete nail scrapers, two Allen key scrapers.

easily. General emptying can be done with the lathe running, but be careful—too much pressure will wreck the piece, especially once its walls are thin. You'll need to stop the lathe occasionally to empty shavings, and you will even need to take your piece off the lathe at times to shake out the residue.

Working through an opening of about 7mm (photo 3), hollowing is done more by feel and intuition. You soon get a feel for where the top of the tool is and for roughly how thick the vessel's walls are, but you can check in a number of ways. The method I prefer is to insert a small light into the vessel. Wet, light-coloured timbers will literally glow once wall thickness of 1mm or so is achieved (photo 4).

I alternate between the straight scraper and another with a slightly bent shaft to hollow the bulk of the form. To get into the more difficult undercut area just beneath the neck of the vessel, I switch to a scraper made from an old Allen key, shortened and ground with a round nose. With its tip at right angles to the shaft, it's easy to get into difficult areas, however it takes time to get a feel for this tool. A couple of Allen keys of different lengths should enable access to almost any tight spot—in fact I do nearly all of my hollowing with three scrapers.

Obviously, each turner will develop his or her own technique to suit their needs. Some turners use a vacuum cleaner with a nozzle tip as a blower to remove shavings from their vessels. Some have been known to run their lathes is reverse so they can cut on the side opposite them, looking into the vessel as they work. Also, if you work in a darkened room, it is easier to see where wood needs to be removed, as light is more visible in thinner parts of the vessel.

Once I've turned the interior to about 1mm wall thickness, I reduce the size of the base and complete sanding. The vessel is then carefully parted off, using my left hand to support it before it breaks free. The remaining stub is then carved away with a carving gouge and hand sanded. This finished form measured 45mm diameter by 50mm high, and weighed just a few grams.

2

3

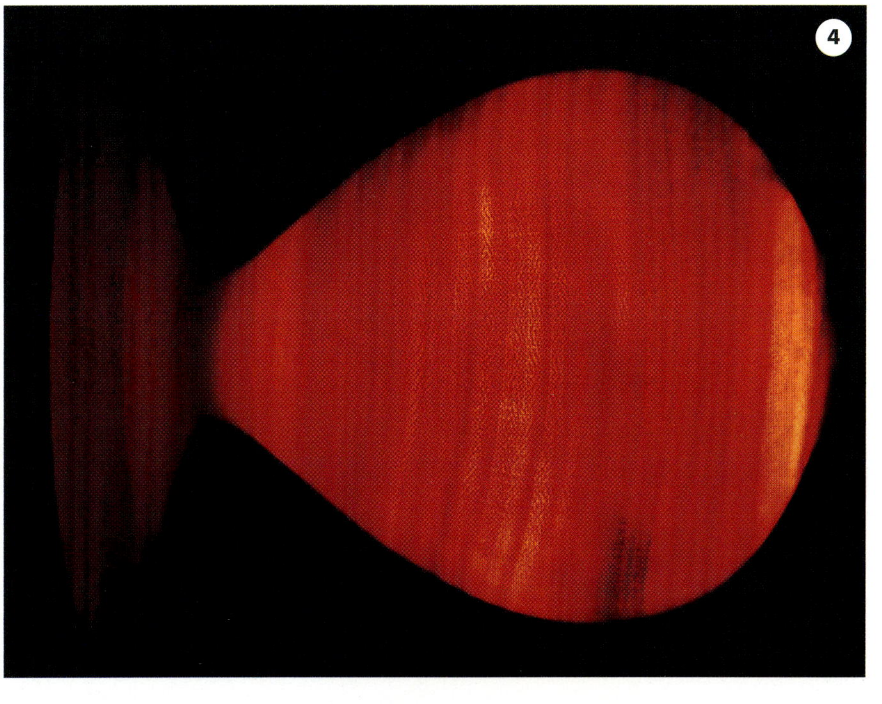
4

A Box of Spillikins

'Seven Equal Pieces' was a feature in Australian Wood Review #16 which presented the work of seven leading turners, each of whom was given a same-sized piece of Huon pine to turn. Richard Raffan chose to turn the spillikins and box pictured. Here's how he did it...

What couldn't I do with a block of Huon pine! Initially I thought this would be a good chance to see how many dozen small boxes I could get from one piece, cleaving the block (rather than sawing) to save valuable material and using every last scrap. The wood would need to be very dense and resinous, not to mention straight grained. But I soon remembered that I'd be pushed for time, having a lecture tour only weeks away, and so I opted for a project which would be less time consuming.

Bowls were definitely out: too obvious, and anyway this was an opportunity to do something a bit different to my normal production. Soon enough I decided to make a set of spillikins—for the game commonly referred to as 'pick-up-sticks', and as many boxes as I could manage from the remainder of the blank.

Spillikin sets are a sort of slow production item for me (I've sold around 115 sets since 1978) so I know I need top quality straight-grained material, especially for the sticks. A set consists of 35 turned and carved sticks in a box. I used to make fifty sticks, but found the game more enjoyable with fewer. Contrary to general perception, the spillikins, usually 190mm long, are comparatively easy to make. They are a great skew chisel exercise, demanding minimal tool pressure against the wood and axis.

The box is the difficult bit. You can drill out the inside, but for a really good job the internal endgrain has to be hand-turned. And finishing the external endgrain will push your technical skills to the limit too.

Usually I make the box with a suction fit lid, which slides over a 25-30mm flange on the base. I always make the box first, then make sticks exactly the right length for that particular box. A box with an internal diameter of 40mm should accommodate 25 spillikins with ease, but with harder woods like gidgee or mulga I can make the sticks thin enough to fit within a 35mm diameter.

When the wood finally arrived only a couple of days before I was due to go overseas, I was disappointed to find the block barely large enough for what

1

2

3

4

5

6

7

8

9

10

11

I had in mind. The block was only 200mm square and a blank for a box with a suction fit lid needs to be at least 230mm long. However there was enough of the straight-grained dense resinous material I look for in Huon pine for the sticks.

With the material limited, I opted for a threaded lid on a 10mm long flange. This 10mm added to the 5mm needed at either end of the box (the thickness of the lid and base) meant that the spillikins could only be 180mm long at most.

Making the Box

The box is best made first, following standard procedures. It is the depth to which both lid and base are hollowed that makes this a testing project. Ensuring that the grain runs the length of the blank, cut one 50mm square (photo 1).

At the same time, and as near parallel to the axis as possible, cut about forty 10mm squares for the sticks (photo 2). (I expect some breakages due to grain defects even if I manage to get through without a major catch.) The blanks were cut from the denser, more resinous and darker material seen on the upper side of the blank.

Turn a short tenon to fit your chuck and true the blank to a cylinder (photo 3). Part off the base section. Note that the shoulder will seat on the chuck jaw rim, whilst it identifies the bottom of the base, enabling you to ensure that the grain alignment in the box remains as it was in the tree (photo 4). True the lid section prior to hollowing (photo 5). Drill a depth hole leaving 5-8mm for the top of the lid.

Hollow using no more than 5mm of the left corner of a square-end scraper. The tape on the tool blade marks the depth required (photo 6). Sand and finish the inside of the lid.

Before cutting the thread on such a soft timber I flow thin cyanoacrylate adhesive (*Superglue*) over the surface to harden the wood. I use a *Klein* threading jig and a 60° cutter to cut the thread (photo 7).

Establish the approximate diameter of the base flange which will fit into the lid. The lid should just fit over the end of the flange. If you fit the lid on tight at this stage, chances are it won't fit properly when the job is finished. Hollow the base before fitting the lid. This is especially important if you are making a suction fit lid. Use your hand to dampen the vibration as the cut proceeds. Again, the tape on the blade marks the required depth (photo 8).

Harden the flange with cyanoacrylate glue, then cut the thread, or fit the lid on tight if you are going for a suction fit (photo 9). Sand the inside. For most of us the base is too deep to sand by hand, so use abrasive wrapped around a dowel (photo 10). With the inside of the box completed, screw the lid to the base (photo 11) and complete the outside (photo 12).

Making the Spillikins

When making the sticks be sure not to have all the beads in the same area; they won't fit into the box! I make six sets each of five picking and lifting sticks with sharp and curved ends. Spillikin blanks need to be gripped (here in a scroll chuck with long jaws) rather than mounted between centres (photo 13). Lay out the length of the spillikin. Photo 14 shows the spillikin being turned using a 15mm skew chisel. Flat sections of the spillikins are shaped on a small disc sander.

A set of spillikins is the stuff of heirlooms. The are not easy to make but should nevertheless be within the capabilities of any turner who proceeds with care. During hands-on workshops I have cajoled dozens of novice turners into making at least one stick and surprising themselves.

If you really cannot manage to turn the inside of the box or find the external endgrain just too difficult, make up a square section box. The spillikin sticks are an ideal project to work away at, making three or four at a time until you have a set. In no time you'll be surprised at how well you can handle a 15mm skew chisel.

Natural Edged Platter

Andrew Potocnik was sent a billet of prickly acacia from outback Western Queensland to turn and had to work within the contraints of the material and a very short time frame.

There I was with half a log of a timber I'd never encountered before, accompanied with a brief I'd somehow aligned myself to, presenting me with an extremely tight time-line within which to work. I had no choice but to set about eliminating my first and foremost problem—that of examining the material I was to work with, hoping to create a piece which would do justice to its positive qualities, as well as making the most of less-wanted characteristics. I also needed to create an object which may well be exhibited in the future.

Unwrapping a modern-day sarcophagus of plastic and wrapping tape, I eventually found a preserved half log of prickly acacia or *Acacia nilotica*. On initial inspection it didn't seem to lend itself to stock standard forms. Although my sample proved to be visually interesting, my greatest challenge came from major heart checking, exposed after cutting the log. If I'd chosen to cut away all imperfections I would have had to penetrate almost a quarter of the way into the log, and then been left with nothing but spindle turning material.

A near impossible time-line needed an immediate solution. There was no time to think, but with a backlog of ideas my cranial computer would surely find the answer. Thankfully, during the course of a mind-clearing run, I connected a recent concept to the brief. My design would explore the interaction of a flat surface with a turned bowl form elevated on legs. It was almost half a log, around 170mm wide, 100mm deep and 400mm long, with cracks penetrating approximately 30mm into it. I intended to exploit its interesting backsawn face, pale sapwood and bark edges, as well as the grain exposed by turning into the log.

Photo 1 shows the log with a rough sketch incorporating curved outer edges, which were later modified to prevent clashing with the log's natural curve, allowing inclusion of natural edges in the final design.

Cutting the log open I found the cracks were far worse than anticipated, the timber far greener than expected, but the colour exquisite and resembling fine Macassar ebony.

With a faceplate fixed to the eventual opening of the bowl, I roughed its underside. Photo 2 shows the form with a foot which would be gripped in a scroll chuck, later to be removed. The slight curve in the rectangular section of the bowl created an oriental feel, which would be echoed in the handles. A V-line cut was made to leave a clear demarcation of planes, especially in the event of heavy sanding.

Reversed in a scroll chuck, the top was turned to match curved sections, exposing backsawn sections of the log.

In hollowing the bowl section I found that this timber blunted my gouges fairly quickly, although it was easily cut, as most green timbers are. A scraper was effectively used to refine the forms.

The main photo shows the large split which ran through the log's core. Without prior experience of this timber I was naturally concerned as to what would happen as the wood dried.

Once I was satisfied with the final form, the exposed surface was dried with a heat gun, then sanded. The flat surfaces were easily sanded by hand on the stationary lathe. The striped grain resembled African zebrano.

Photo 3 shows the form reversed onto a jam fit carrier enabling removal of the stub by which it had previously been held. As the supporting rim had some fine cracks, I made the carrier a little loose and relied on heat-sensitive glue to fix it in place. Too much pressure might have caused the bowl form to split and possibly destroy the whole piece.

Stock for legs and handles was cut (photo 4), ready for rough turning, and allowed an opportunity to test the spindle turning qualities of this timber. In its green state, side grain *Acacia nilotica* again performed wonderfully, allowing sharp tools to leave a smooth surface with a scent which reminded me of blackwood.

The short time-frame of this project meant the piece couldn't simply be left to dry. The rough-turned components were therefore microwaved to be later completed. In order to establish equilibrium moisture content (EMC) I measured the weight of the wood prior to and following heating on several occasions. When the weight had stabilised I assumed EMC had been attained.

The process of drying timber can cause significant cell distortion, however here there was little change. Existing cracks seemed to not worsen, however they still needed to be stabilised, or bonded in a way which would blend with the completed piece. A friend convinced me to experiment with black coloured resin.

The ends of the bowl were shaped to a curve which would be mirrored in the line of the handles. Whilst shaping, I became convinced that dried prickly acacia was much harder than expected. Maybe this was the result of microwave drying. Although noticeably harder, the dry timber still worked well both on side and endgrain, scraped or cut.

Photo 5 shows how the finished handles follow the curved ends of bowl, which varied in width. Space between the two forms wasn't intended to be uniform, but increased toward the ends of the handles.

Gripped in a *Vicmarc* scroll chuck the legs were turned from dried material to a simple curved taper. A 4mm tenon was turned on the end of each leg which fitted into a corresponding hole drilled into the flat section of the bowl (see photo 6). The legs were intended to not clash visually with other parts of the form.

Using a specially made jig which allows compound angled settings, holes were drilled on a compound angle which allowed legs to be splayed when viewed side or end on. The angle was almost square to the face of adjoining faces, which allowed for perfect matching at intersecting sections.

To the fit handles, I fell back on my stock standard 2mm stainless steel rods as the means of connecting the components. Using a 'V-block' on a pedestal drill to establish parallel holes in the handles, I still needed to figure out a way of drilling corresponding holes into the edge of the bowl.

Photo 7 shows the highly technical device used to solve this problem! A *Dremel*, off-cuts, veneer scraps for packing and clamps enabled me to drill on a consistent angle simply by rotating the bowl and 'eye-balling' parallel angles.

Once the piece was assembled and the glue allowed to dry, an oil finish was used to highlight colour and grain. My current choice of oil finishes, *Organoil*, was flooded on and then allowed to soak in and harden before being wiped back to reveal the beauty of *Acacia nilotica*. Rich blacks and golden browns convinced me that this is a timber worthy of further exploration, providing that this sample doesn't represent typical negative qualities of this species. If it does, we'll need to again re-evaluate our expectations of a valuable resource.

Laminating Blanks From Scrap

Recycling timber offcuts into laminated turning blanks is a satisfying way of creating large and interesting stock while making the most of your timber resource, writes Andrew Potocnik.

When laminating, I like to highlight the fact that wood has been joined, rather than trying to make it look like one big piece of solid wood. It's nearly impossible to totally disguise a glue joint, so I usually laminate a piece of contrasting veneer into the joint to accent it instead. I generally use veneers that I've collected over the years, mainly scraps, but you could cut your own veneers. Varying their thickness also adds another design option.

Woodturners usually cut their turning blanks from square blocks of wood, leaving four triangular scraps. Photo 1 shows how these can be rearranged into a small block which can then be

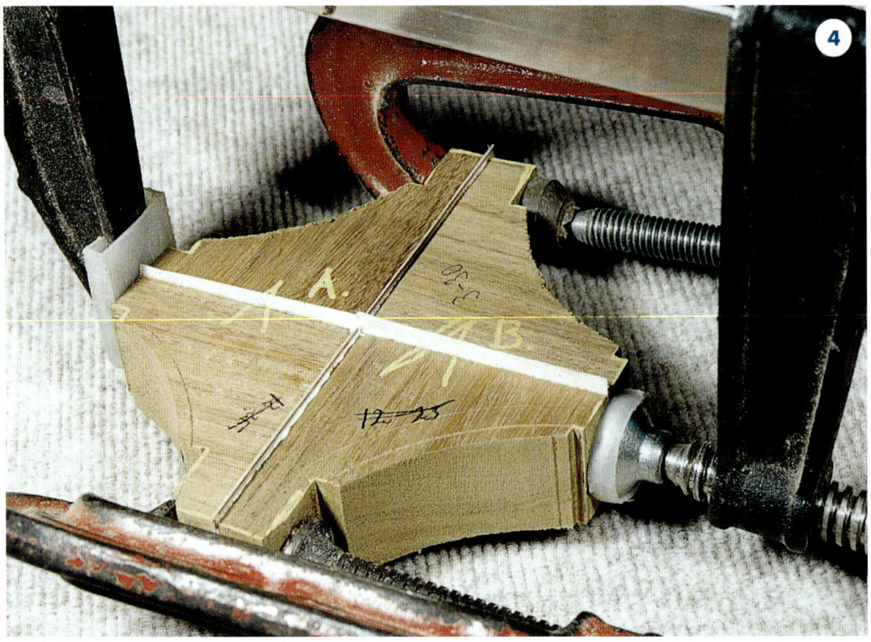

turned. Consider how you line up the grain and try to use this as a feature too. Photo 2 shows an arrangement of opposing grain with veneer inserted. Gluing intersecting lines can be a problem as the wood tends to slip a little when being clamped. Simple jigs can overcome this problem, however an alternative is to intentionally off-set the lines to create a pattern.

Plane or sand each surface to be glued. I use a shop-built disc sander attachment which I made for my lathe. To check for flatness, hold the two pieces you're joining up to the light. If you can see light through any part of the joint, re-sand. If you can't correct the surface, use an epoxy resin glue, such as *Araldite*, which acts as a gap filler and adhesive. Note that the resulting thicker glue line may look unsightly on light coloured timbers, but will not be as noticeable on darker timbers.

Photo 3 shows one half glued and clamped. The excess glue that has squeezed out along the join indicates that the faces are meeting correctly. Be sure to cover each face fully, spreading the glue over the full surface to ensure proper bonding. I've used PVA glue here and find it sufficiently strong for this type of work. When tightening the clamps, don't overdo it, or else you run the risk of weakening the joint. You will notice that I've also written the time of clamping onto the wood. If you're gluing a series of blocks, this helps you to know when they're ready to be unclamped. Once dry, sand the faces that will be glued next, cut your veneer, cover the faces to be joined and clamp together (photo 4)—note that I've cut new notches for the clamps to fit into.

I next decided to create an elliptical line around the perimeter of the bowl. A diagonal line was cut through the block and a piece of veneer glued in (photo 5). You can also see how the vertical lines didn't meet perfectly, reinforcing the point I made earlier about the problems associated with movement while clamping.

Safety

It is important to ensure that all joints are securely glued with a sufficiently strong glue before you start turning.

The centrifugal forces generated by a lathe at high speed can be enormous and a bad glue joint may not be capable of standing up to this force.

The Turning

Use a compass to mark a circle and cut the blank and bandsaw to the line (photo 6). Turn your blank in the usual way. An easy way to mount the blank is to attach it to a carrier (a piece of scrap timber screwed onto a faceplate) using heat sensitive glue or double-sided carpet tape. To locate it on the carrier, line up the tailstock centre with the hole formed by the compass when marking the circle (photo 7). Apply a series of dots of hot glue to the carrier and press the blank into position. Wait a few seconds for the glue to cool and set and you're ready to go.

Turn the outside of the bowl through to its finished state, including a clearly defined foot or base. Use a chisel to lever the bowl from its carrier, then reverse and remount it. Cut a rebate just a whisker broader than the diameter of the bowl's foot into the carrier just used. Apply hot glue to the rebate and press the bowl into place. If all has gone according to plan, the bowl should be perfectly centred and firmly fixed. Hollow out the inside, keeping in mind that it is sometimes worth supporting the bowl with the tailstock while removing the bulk of material.

Once shaped, sand the bowl and remove it from the carrier. If you've used glue sparingly, you should be able to remove the bowl by pushing your thumbs between it and the carrier and gently pushing the bowl away. If this doesn't work or the bowl is too thin to allow this, then part it away from the carrier. A little hand sanding to remove any leftover scratches, and the work is ready for you to apply your favourite finish.

You'll find this technique will open up great scope for experimentation, whether pre-planned or spontaneous. Patterns can arranged according to timber grain, colour, segment size and shape. If you're not already an exponent of full-scale segmented work you may now be tempted to try.

5

6

7

Laminated Construction

This project by Gary Beck creates a bowl around 110mm high and 300mm wide from a piece of wood which is only 25mm thick to start with. The beauty of this method is that there is minimal timber waste and considerable scope for design variation.

This project teaches you how to literally think outside the 'four-square'. Follow the steps photo by photo and you will soon be able to adapt this technique to create more from less.

1

1. Start with a piece of timber 150mm x 25mm x 600mm long. Plane and thickness this accurately on both faces and one long edge.

2. Cut the board in half and clamp the two halves together along the long edge. Find the centre and draw as large a circle as possible with a compass. From this large circle measure and mark inwards four 20mm increments and draw circles at these points.

2

3

3. Set your bandsaw table 45° and cut along the pencil lines. Use a sharp blade and take adequate safety precautions.

4. Cut the last piece with the outside at 90°.

5. You should now have 10 pieces of timber ready to be assembled.

6. Carefully clean up any burrs from the bandsaw and, using a cyanoacrylate adhesive such as *Superglue*, glue the matching halves together on a flat surface. PVA can also be used for this, however the clamping required may be difficult. Cyanoacrylate, on the other hand, sets almost immediately and the segments can be held in place with your hands. (Note the sheet of plastic to protect the machine surface. Although not shown it is advisable to wear protective gloves when using this type of adhesive and make sure you have good ventilation.-)

7. Clean up the circles to eliminate any glue residue and if necessary lightly plane the joints flat. Stack the pieces to form an upside-down bowl, off-

4

5

6

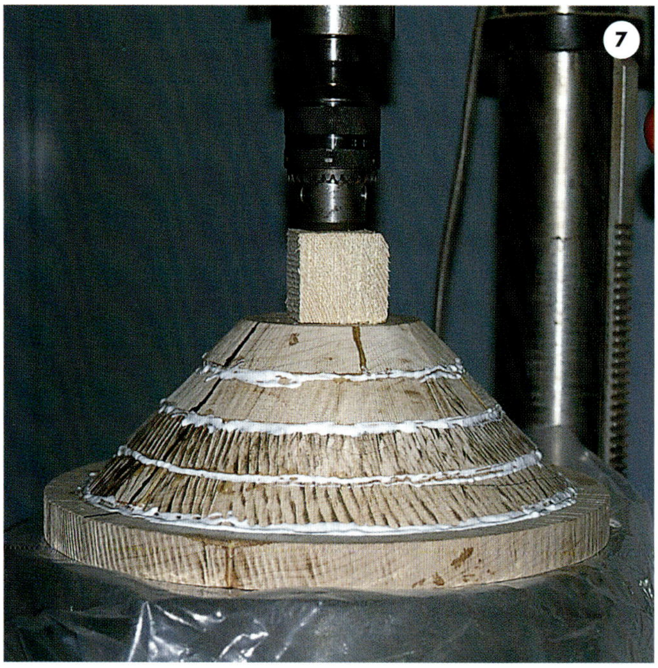

7

8

setting the joints to strengthen the structure and add to its appearance. Mark a line along the stack to ensure the segment order is maintained. Apply PVA to each circle in turn, check for correct alignment and clamp the blank using either weights, the lathe, clamps, or as shown, a drill press. Allow the glue to dry overnight.

8. Mount a plywood disc on the lathe (I drill a hole in the plywood and mount it in a scroll chuck.) True up the disc.

9. Remove the disc from the lathe and mount the bowl blank on the disc, ensuring it is accurately centred. I

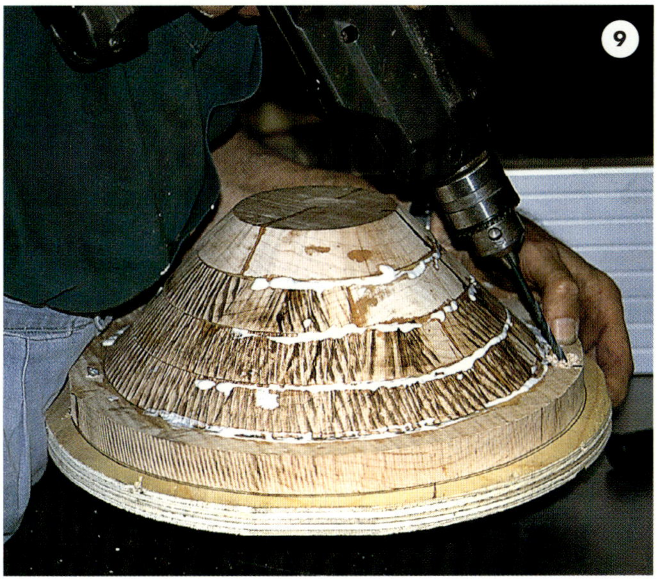

drill six holes and fix the blank with wood screws. The screws are fixed on an angle, which allows the holes to be later turned off without losing any depth from the bowl.

10. Mount the disc with the affixed bowl blank on the lathe and turn a shallow opening on the base to accept the scroll chuck. Attach the scroll chuck to the bowl blank.

11. Re-mount the blank on the lathe with the scroll chuck and, using the tailstock for support, begin turning in the usual way. I turn the outside first, then the inside, after which I re-mount the bowl to clean up the base.

Once you have mastered this technique you will be able to vary the angle of bandsawing from 45° to create different shaped vessels. You can also use contrasting timbers in patterns to create a dynamic effect. Within the contstraints of timber size, glue strength and your skill there are also endless bowls of various diameters that can be turned. What, for instance, would happen if you begin with a piece of timber 300mm x 45mm x 1200mm?

This project was inspired by Dale L. Nish's book 'Creative Woodturning'.

Segmented Form

Once you know how to create laminated turnings, a whole world of geometric and decorative possibilities will open up to you. Ted Anderson explains in easy-to-follow steps how to make this beautiful bowl.

Turning segmented or laminated sections of timber opens up enormous design possibilities. With the variables of section size, species, colour and patterning your turnings can express all your geometric fantasies! But not only must all the usual prerequisites of creating a pleasing form be met, but care must also be taken to precisely calculate, cut and join all the segments of your project.

You must start with a full size drawing, otherwise you may easily lose the plot and finish up with an unexpected result. I use a drawing board and a T-square, but graph paper will also allow you to map an accurate design.

For this project I have made a bowl to illustrate the basic method of segmented turning using the stacked ring method. Figures 1 and 2 overleaf show the bowl in side and plan views. The different coloured blocks denote each ring layer and how they should be overlapped. The dotted lines show the actual size of each wedge, to which I add 2mm to allow for sanding. Each ring has 12 segments (except for the centre bands)—this is the number I usually choose. By dividing 12 into 360° an angle of 30° is arrived at. The side of each segment will be half that—15°.

Step 1

Cut all timber to size, making sure it is oversize for thickness (22mm is ideal). I cut the timber into strips which equal the radial length of each segment. I like to do this at least two weeks in advance and sticker them out in the workshop. The actual cutting size of each segment is referred to as the 'chord'. This is the largest dimension of the segment between each radial line which should include a further 2mm sanding allowance.

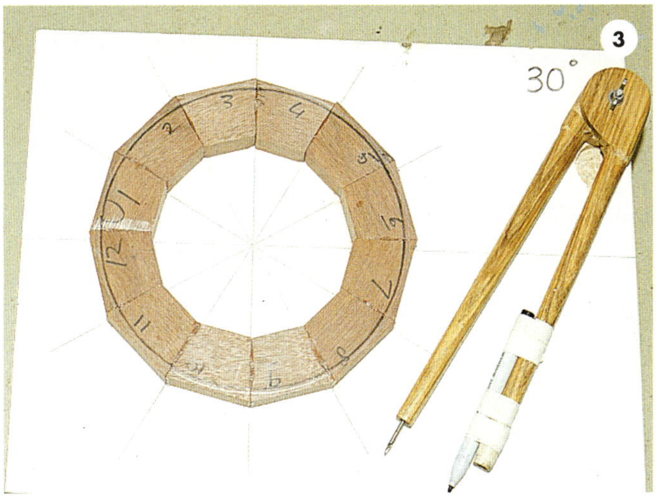

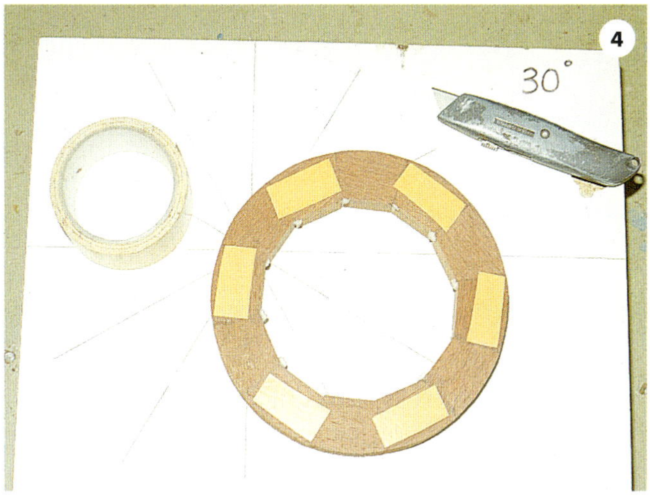

A bandsaw, benchsaw or jigsaw can be used to cut the segments, however I use a tablesaw with a 40-tooth tungsten carbide blade and a sliding protractor, numbering as I go (photo 1—please note the guard has been removed for visual clarity). A block of wood, bolted to the main fence acts as a length stop and, if at least 150mm in front of the blade, prevents the segments jamming against the fence and being thrown at you at high speed. Be very careful to move each segment away from the blade with a pushstick after each cut.

Step 2

I sand the edges of all segments on a disc sander, making sure that the table is at 90° to the sanding face (photo 2). I have made a sliding table on which templates of different angles can be fitted as required.

Test fit segments on a setting out board—they should fit exactly. Glue these together on a piece of melamine to which a diagram of the segments has been drawn. I use a protractor and a permanent felt tipped pen (photo 3). Melamine offcuts can be purchased from most kitchen manufacturers. A liberal dab of glue (I use an adhesive which sets quickly, strongly and with minimal creep) is applied to one of the segments and the next one is rubbed against it exactly into position on the diagram.

Gluing up in numerical order will give a butcher-block arrangement. The excess glue that squeezes out onto the board

Fig.1

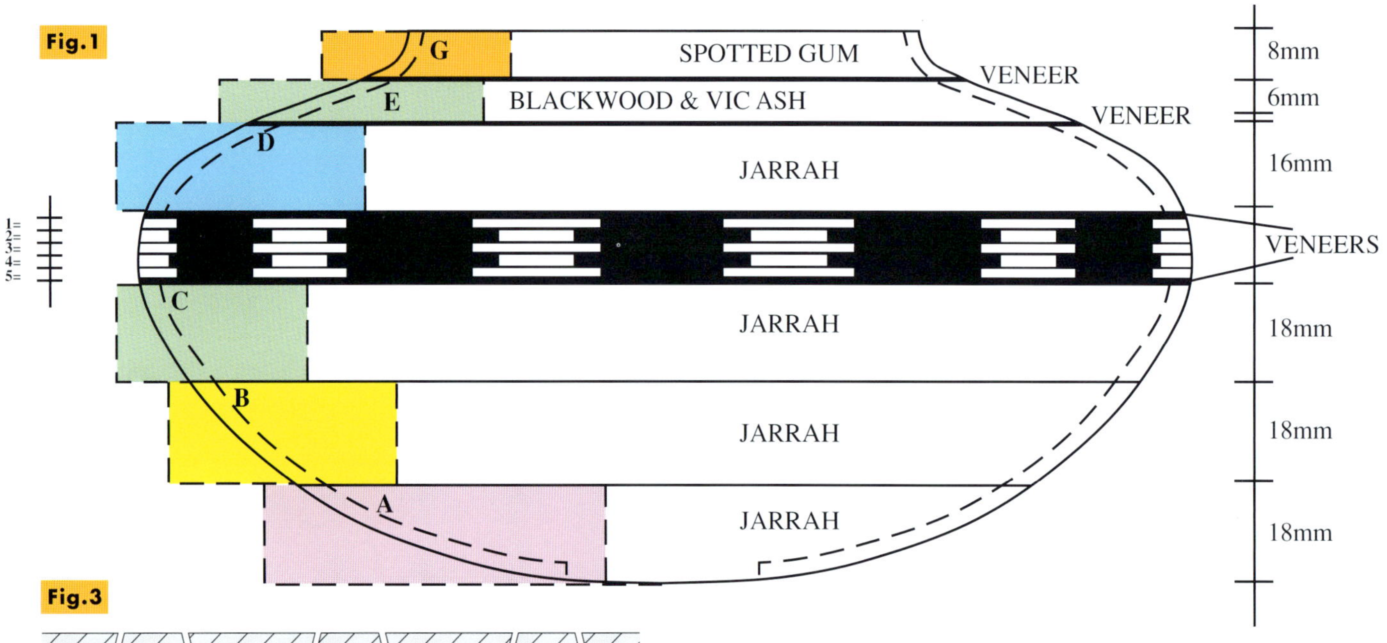

Fig.3

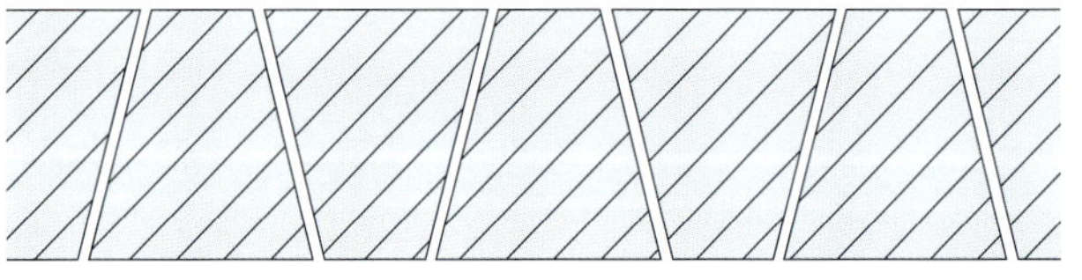

Fig.2

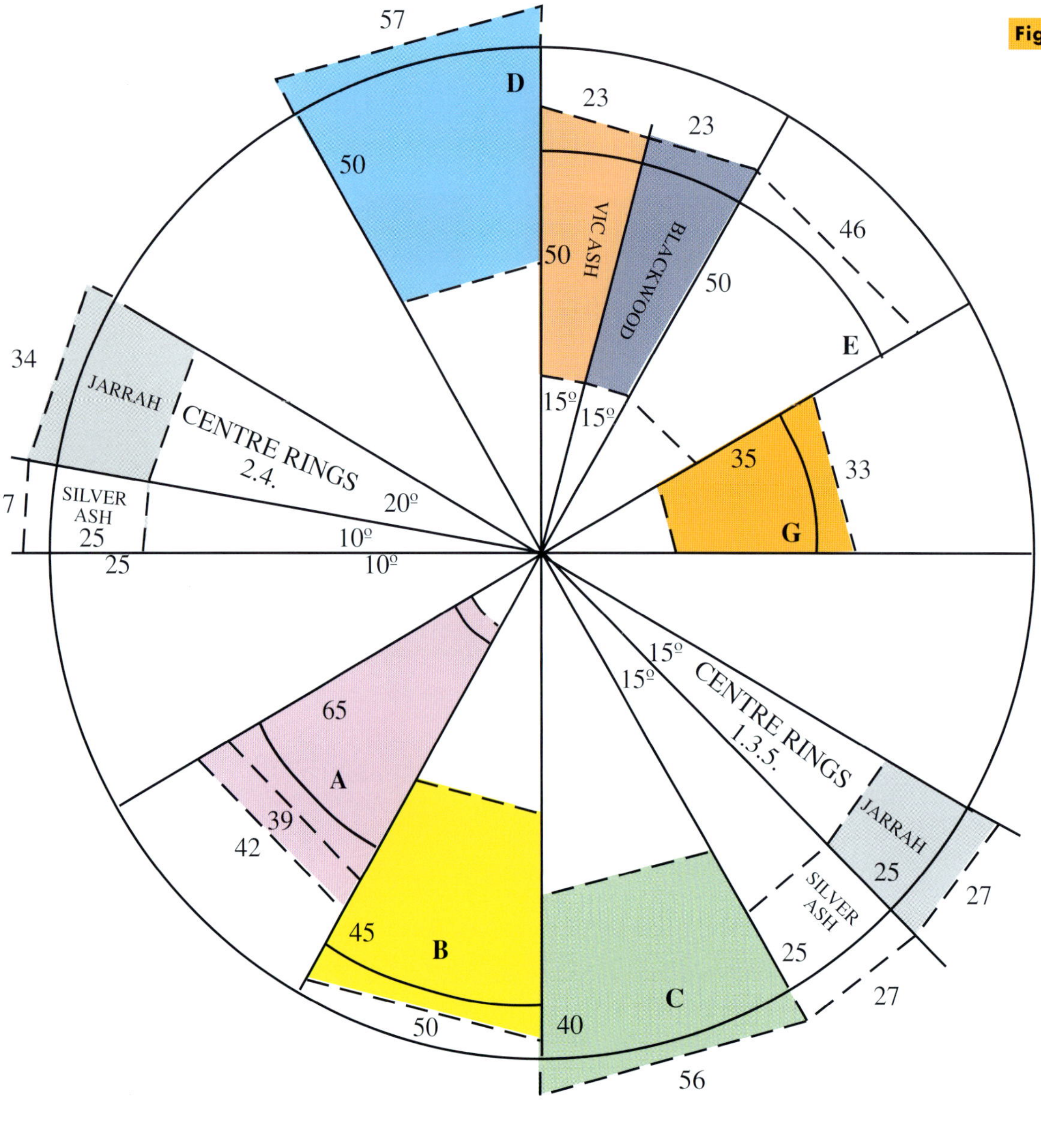

will hold it firm on the board. After the glue has dried use a compass to draw a circle on the ring to the required size. The ring (we'll call this 'ring A') can then be easily prised off with a sharp chisel.

Step 3

Bandsaw or jigsaw closely to the compass line. Cut as near possible to a perfect circle so the ring will line up accurately for the next step.

Step 4

The ring is then fixed to a wooden faceplate with double-sided carpet tape (photo 4). Concentric grooves on the faceplate make it easy to centre the ring accurately. If the ring is off-centre the segments will be sized differently and it will be impossible to line everything up later on.

Step 5

Face off the exposed surface of the ring perfectly flat and turn it to the diameter required. Mark a circle which is the diameter of ring B on the exposed surface (photo 5) in order to position the next ring accurately. It is an advantage if you have another faceplate to turn the B on, so ring A can be left in place. Make ring B face and turn it to the diameter of ring A.

Step 6

Turn off the corner of ring A and then glue ring B to A. A heavy weight will provide sufficient pressure while the

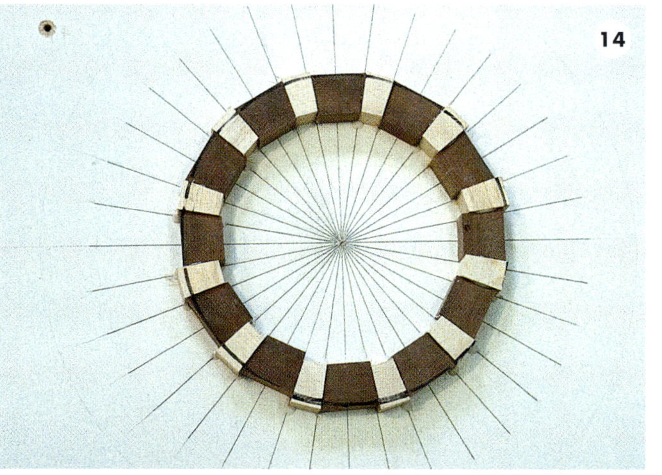

glue dries. Make sure the ring is precisely located and the segments are in a brickwork pattern. When dry, face this ring to 18mm thickness and then mark a circle which is the diameter required for ring C.

Follow the same procedure and when the glue has dried, remount this assembly on the lathe and turn the outside shape of this section (photo 6).

Step 7

Turn out the bottom to receive a plug, making sure that it is parallel (photo 7). Fix a block of selected wood onto a screw chuck and turn a plug to fit the hole, once again checking it is parallel and neat (photo 8). Glue it in place (photo 9) and when dry, the completed lower half of the bowl can be removed from the wooden faceplate and then reversed onto the headstock. You can hold this with a screw or scroll chuck. Turn the inside to the desired thickness (I like a wall thickness of 4-6mm) and then make the face perfectly flat. Remove this section from the headstock and place aside, still attached to the chuck.

Step 8

Make up ring D and, after truing the face, remove it still attached to the faceplate.

Step 9

Photo 10 shows the circles of veneer which must now be cut and glued one by one, (start with the larger ones) to ring D. Alternate the colours, starting with the lighter veneer, and lay each successive circle with the grain at 90° to the previous one. Use a piece of melamine and a weight to glue each veneer circle.

When these are dry remount the assembly on the lathe and turn off the excess on the outside—I use the point of a skew chisel for this. Now you are ready to make the ring of blackwood and Victorian ash. This is made in a similar manner, but with 24 segments (you will have to make another setting out board to suit, the angle will be 7.5°) see photo 11. Remove the ring when dry and face off on the wooden faceplate, then remove and glue to the uppermost veneer layer. When dry, face off to the required thickness and glue the smaller set of veneers to it in the same way as before.

Step 10

Make up the top ring (I used spotted gum) and fit as before. Turn this section, shape the outer wall and rim (photo 12) and remove from the headstock and make a jam-fit chuck to suit the inside diameter of the rim (photo 13). Reverse the top assembly onto the jam chuck and now turn the inner wall.

Step 12

The next step is to make up the centre bands—for this you will need a setting out board using a 10° template. The bands consist of three rings of 24 segments at 15° and two rings of 24 segments. If you look carefully at photo 14 you will see that one segment is at 10° and the other is at 20°.

Step 13

Glue up a ring of each of the above segments using 19mm thick wood and, following the previous procedures, fix each to a wooden faceplate and face

off the outer surface, then part off rings of 4mm thick using a thin parting tool. In photo 15 you can see the rings ready for assembly. Glue ring 1 to the top section and ring 5 to the bottom section. When these are dry face them off to 3mm thick (photo 16). Rings 2 and 4 are then placed in position so that they form the pattern on the final piece, after you have faced these to size you can fit the centre ring to either the top or bottom section so that it lines up with rings 1 and 5.

Step 14

Carefully turn off the excess of the bands on both the inside and outside and make sure the wall thickness is the same top and bottom (photo 17). You can now sand the inner surfaces and finish with a sanding sealer.

Step 15

Join the top and bottom (note the revolving tail centre in photo 18). The bowl is ready to final turn and finish sand and you can part off the plug on the bottom (photo 19) and finish this section (photo 20).

Step 16

After sanding to at least 400 grit, the bowl can be removed from the lathe and a jam chuck made to suit the plug in the bottom. The bowl can then be mounted and held in position with a dowel and a piece of rag to protect the inside from scratches (photo 21). The rim can now be finished and the bowl removed and oiled or waxed, as you prefer.

I personally enjoy creating and turning laminated forms with this method. I hope my explanation will give you the opportunity to experiment with this technique.

Divided and Joined

Faced with a turning challenge, Andrew Potocnik's unique response was to create a piece which was turned, segmented and assembled with a contrasting detail.

A piece of Huon pine arrived in the post from *Australian Wood Review*. The instructions were simple: 'Turn anything you wish but use the maximum amount of the blank possible. You may divide it and use other techniques of sculpting or surface ornamentation, but no other materials may be incorporated. Simple!? Normally I begin a new piece by developing a design and selecting the materials best suited to it. I then experiment with the scale to establish the right proportions. This set of instructions however, forced me to work in reverse.

The key to completing this piece successfully was to plan carefully, developing drawings from which to work. The enlargement and reduction function of the photocopier is an invaluable aid for scaling drawings. I decided on a bowl which would be quartered and then reassembled with a cross-section dissecting the bowl. This would in turn form a stand on which the completed piece could rest. I had been thinking about this idea for a while and planned to use two contrasting timbers for the major components. For this project I would have to use a different technique to contrast the parts. I do not find Huon pine a particularly suitable material for most of my work, and didn't feel it would be the best material for this

piece. I knew it would be possible to achieve the outcome I had in mind, but only with some mental effort. This is the type of challenge I enjoy, so I set about creating a design within the restrictions imposed.

The assemblage that I had in mind required a fair bit of cutting, which presented me with my first moral dilemma. I felt guilty about cutting up a nice big piece of Huon pine. I even thought about working out the volume of wood available and substituting it with other pieces of smaller dimensions!

Once the planning stage was over I established how much timber would be needed for the rings that are used to make the legs—these would come from a slice of the blank. The actual bowl blank was cut with the bandsaw table tilted so as to reduce waste (photo 1). With the blank mounted on the lathe, I roughed it down to the required shape using a template as a guide (photo 2).

The outside was not sanded at this stage. Next, the shell of the bowl was separated from the faceplate using a *Stewart System* lance, which left me with a hollowed bowl form and a stub attached to the faceplate, which could be used later.

I now had to transfer the shell onto a carrier which had been turned from a scrap piece of timber. The bowl was then glued into the carrier, and its interior turned out to the required shape (photo 3) and sanded through to its completed stage.

Using a parting tool, I separated the bowl from its carrier. Having planned ahead, I turned a step outside the holding rebate and marked it prior to gluing. Photo 4 shows the 12mm marking on the carrier. This would later remind me how far I would need to cut to separate the two.

After this, I needed to create a carrier that would allow access to the exterior portion of the bowl to complete it. A push fit carrier seemed the best choice. Progress on the shaping was monitored using the template created earlier.

Once completed, I used a straight edge and fine pencil to mark out sections of the bowl which would be cut away on the bandsaw (photo 5). Photo 6 shows the cut bowl revealing approximately 3mm of wall thickness throughout most of the form. After some drawing and measuring I established the required thickness and diameter of the ring that would be cut to form the legs.

In keeping with the spirit of this exercise, I had set aside a slice from the bottom of the block to use for this ring, however, I found that it would be possible to obtain the required material from other scrap material. Careful consideration was given to the direction of the growth rings, aiming to reduce problems associated with feather grain, which would make the ring too fragile.

Photo 7 shows the ring glued with epoxy resin (the arrows indicate grain direction) and the carrier is marked with guide lines that indicate where the ring should be placed so that it is

centred. It was then attached using heat sensitive glue.

Vernier calipers were used to check if the ring had been turned to the right dimension (photo 8). This instrument also makes is possible to see whether the inside and outside edges of the ring are parallel.

Once correctly dimensioned, the ring was shaped on one side, burnt and rubbed back. After reversing, the same was done to the other side. And what do you think happens when you get the slightest catch? You begin to search for the missing pieces and start all over again. Don't forget, it's always important to wear a face shield while using machinery. This time I could have received a serious facial injury had I not been wearing a full face shield, as I always do when turning.

Photos 9 and 10 show the ring before and after burning and cutting into four segments. Slits were filed to accept the quarter ring segments (photo 11).

In order to get an overall idea of how things were shaping up I used some scrap blocks and an old film container to support the various parts as they would be assembled (photo 12). In this way I could see if any changes needed to be made.

Once satisfied things were progressing well, it was time to decide how to connect the legs and bowl, I already had ideas before I began, however ideas don't always work in reality. At this point the bowl was very fragile as there was little remaining wood holding it together. The legs were intended to bind sections together and give the bowl strength.

After fruitlessly exploring some possibilities that would work visually and structurally, I solved the problem during an 18 kilometre run. Models were used to establish the dimensions and shape of the last components of the piece to be made.

Photo 13 shows the 'platelets' that were hand shaped and then glued into place (photo 14). Slots for the platelets were cut into the legs. The ends of the legs were then trimmed to size, burnt (photo 15), then fitted. Finally the bowl and legs were sealed before being glued together.

Wave-Edged Bowl

Wave-edged bowls are one of Stephen Hughes' best known and best selling trademarks. The free-flowing curves are achieved by carving onto a turned form.

The illusion of a 'warped' or waved edge can be created by carving onto a turned form. The beauty of this method is that the edge can be 'waved' as far as the total depth of the blank allows. Endless variations of line are possible. When these forms are combined with added-on bases, stands, feet and spikes, not to mention texture and surface ornamentation, the possibilities are endless.

The wave-edged bowl is created with a blending of skills. Design and choice of timber are important as always, however the marrying of techniques is critical—the viewer's eye should not be aware of the start and end of the turning and the carving. I have applied this technique to bowls with diameters as small as 120mm up to 650mm in my 'Wind Walker' and 'Manta' series. Here is a step-by-step outline of how I design and make a wave-edged bowl.

1. Select a suitable bowl blank. For this project I have used a piece of Huon pine 300 x 50mm in size, however any timber that turns and carves well could be used. Note any faults or natural features that could affect the final design (photo 1). The size of the blank will, to some extent, determine how difficult this type of carved bowl will be. As a guide, I like to make the carved section at least as wide as the turned bowl area of the piece, and the total diameter no smaller than 150mm to make the carving process relatively easy.

2. Draw several side views of the type of edge you would like to attempt. I normally do these to scale by simply sketching a rectangular side view of the blank and then drawing in the various flowing shapes I want to achieve.

Before you commit to the design you want, consider the type and sizes of carving tools you plan to use, any faults or features you want to remove or retain on the edge, how thin you want to make the carving and what style of bowl base you want.

3. Fix the blank (with the bowl facing the tailstock) to the faceplate, or as in photo 1, on a centre screw held in a 4-jaw chuck. Turn the blank true before turning the underside profile of the bowl as shown in photo 2. A ring of timber can be parted away and saved if you wish (photo 3).

When turning the base, turn a 90° stepped section for refixing the bowl into the jaw chuck or a turned female timber chuck for gluing. If you plan to add on or carve feet on the bottom of the bowl you will have to allow enough timber for this. At this stage surfaces are left with a tool finish (photos 4 and 5).

4. Remount the bowl with the upper side now facing towards the tail end of the lathe (photo 6).

5. Turn the upper side of the bowl skirt. Note the way the upper and lower surfaces taper in towards the bowl opening and use figure eight calipers or similar to check the thickness of the narrowest sections (photo 7).

6. Now turn the inside of the bowl. (You may save the bowl centre here if you wish—I use the *Kel McNaughton* system for this.) Again, note the wall thickness using figure eight calipers as you complete the internal shape (photo 8). Try to undercut the top edge of the bowl and also keep it raised by turning its outer surface tapering down and flowing into the outer skirt. This will give the bowl opening a defined line, as well as giving depth to the bowl itself.

7. Sand the internal surface—I like to take all finished surfaces to 600 grit.

8. Now draw the lines for the carving onto the outer edge of the skirt. I attempt to be as accurate as I can here, yet still try to obtain a softness to the line I want. Practise your lines before you begin. On this bowl I wanted to have a finished skirt with a 4mm thickness (photo 9).

9. Using the indexing pin on the lathe to hold the work in position, start to carve the upper side of the skirt. As you progress around the surface you will need to move the indexing pin.

There are several methods which can be used to carve the skirt. Here are some of the ones I use.

Carving with Gouges

Success here relies on sharp tools and a competant understanding of grain direction. I find this technique the most satisfying and reasonably quick, once you have learnt how the tools will behave on the type of timber you have selected. Of course this is why I select timbers that both carve and turn easily (photo 10).

Power Carving

Here an angle grinder fitted with a circular cutter (such as the *Rotary Chisel* shown, or an *Arbortech*) is used (photo 11). This is by far the fastest method of timber shaping I know next to a chainsaw. Safety is the main concern with this method and it is essential that you follow the manufacturer's instructions. You must always wear eye protection or better still a full face shield. For your health you should also protect yourself from the noise and from the finer air borne dust produced. Remember to check your method of holding the piece is strong, as occasional catches will tear a poorly secured piece right off the lathe. Always hold the angle grinder with both hands until it has stopped, and hold it so the circular cutter works off the edge. Never cut in towards the edge or you will most certainly tempt disaster.

Like all timber cutting techniques the cleanest, smoothest results will rely on your ability to go with the grain wherever possible. Although I prefer the quiet satisfaction of hand carving I tend to use this power carving technique to rough out the shape of most of my work, simply because of its speed.

Rotary Burrs

Another power carving technique is to use rotary burrs of all shapes and sizes. These are available in high speed steel, tungsten carbide and diamond impregnated tips. For this project I used a diamond tipped 8mm round burr. To drive the burr I use a *Dremel* drill (there are many types of high speed drills and die grinders suitable for this).

Rotary burrs are great for reaching the more difficult areas of a carving, in this case the deeper undercut waves are so much easier to get into and shape. Spinning at 25,000 revolutions per minute the burrs, when sharp, cut so cleanly that even against the grain cutting is

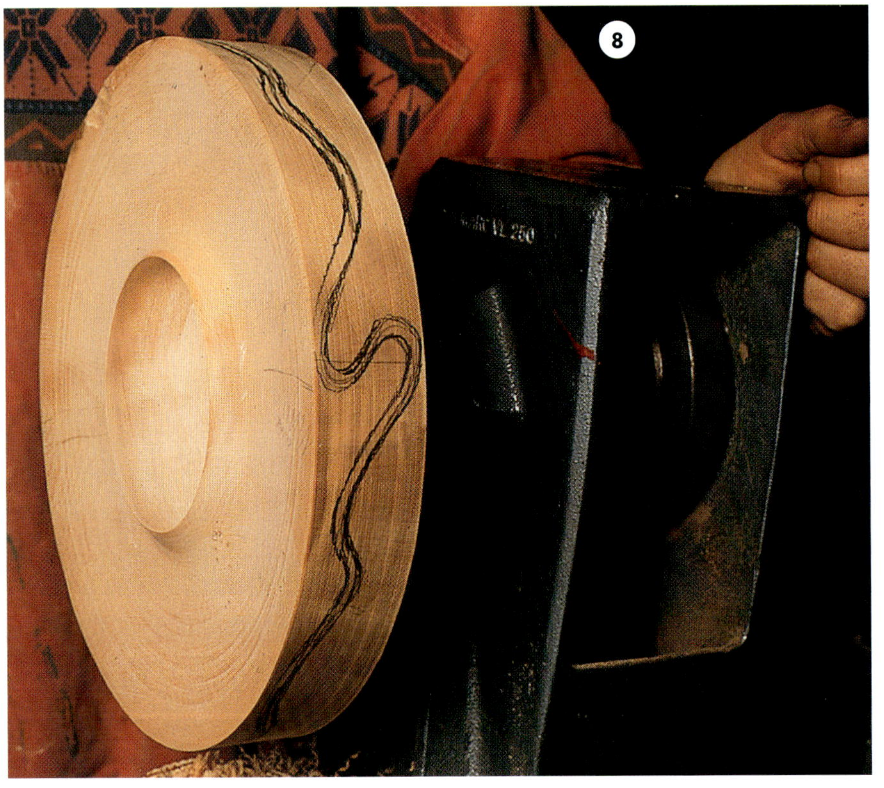

acceptably smooth (photo 12).

The key to achieving even, smooth surfaces with this type of machine is to practise a light gliding motion and avoid heavy pressure cuts when finishing. Again, it is essential that you follow the health and safety precautions I mentioned above for the angle grinder when using any high speed cutting tools.

Of course you don't need to use any power tools to carve this or any other timber project—it's just that they make the process quick and easy but by no means as satisfying as mastering hand carving techniques.

10. Once the top is shaped, start carving the underside of the skirt. If you find it difficult to access the underside you may have to flip the piece over onto the turned stepped block over which the internal rim of the bowl should fit snugly. Note: use the tailstock to hold the bowl onto the stepped block—I do this later anyway to finish off the base. Take the carved surface to about 8-10mm thickness and try to keep it even, judge this by eye at this stage.

11. The final shaping and smoothing of the carved edge is achieved using both hand sanding (photo 13) and disc sanding techniques (photo 14). I use cloth-backed abrasives and a 50mm velcro-faced disc pad which allows quick changing of new abrasive discs. Any lightweight drill can be used to drive these discs, however I prefer a right angle drill for its ease of manoeuvrability.

Firstly remove and blend uneven surfaces with a 80 grit x 50mm disc and then hand sand with 80 grit to remove the facets left from the disc. Repeat this process through each of the following grits: 120, 150, 180, 240, 320, 400. Rub the final surface down with 600 grit. On both sides you need to fade the carved edge into the turned surface of the bowl so they blend into one another.

I try to give an even thickness to the

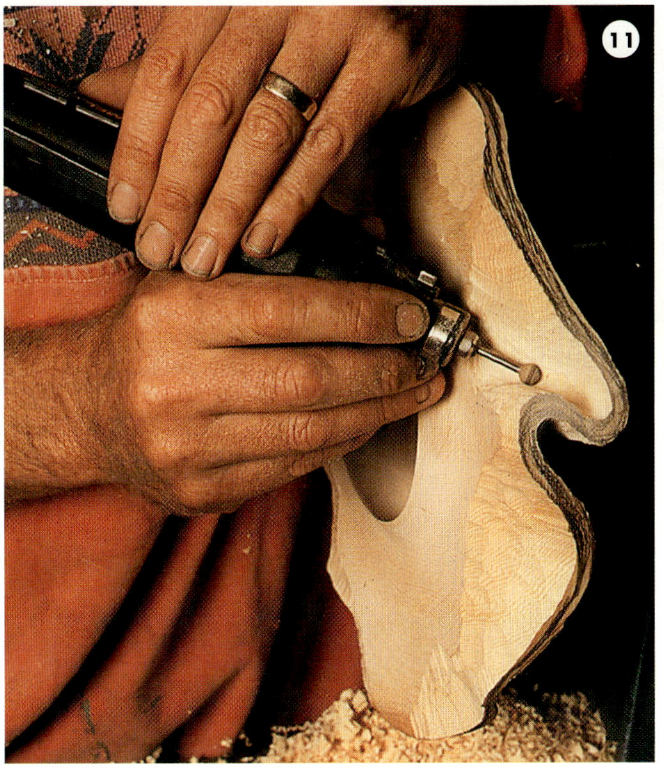

wave-edge and constantly check it, using either a bright light (pale timbers when thinned become translucent) measuring with calipers if I'm unsure as I get towards the final thickness. On this piece I took the wall thickness down to 4mm but I suggest that if you are not familiar with this type of carving you should keep it to around 6mm or more to start with and progress to thinner edges next time.

12. How a piece like this stands can make a huge difference to its appearance. Raising a piece on three feet is a common device on all manner of bowl forms. On these wave-edged pieces the addition of legs gives a creature-like look.

Once the wavy edge is finished it's time to shape the base of the bowl. A standard flat base can be effective, however you may choose to shape it otherwise.

I hope this project inspires you to wave goodbye to the thought that turning is the only way to make a bowl!

Planet Spheres

Stephen Hughes shows you how to turn a celestial body.

Since the dawn of time man has been attracted to the mysteries of the stars and planets. One of my most popular production turnings has had a Saturn-like form which evolved by combining spherical turnings with carved surfaces. In 1980 I had purchased some branch section Huon pine between 50-200mm in diameter. For several years I turned pieces from those sections but had to turn off the small cracks in the sapwood edge to get a sound form from the heartwood. I was disappointed with the amount of timber I was turning into shavings and the small sized blanks I was harvesting from the branches.

I sketched until I came up with a design that enabled me to keep the full cross section of the branch and still obtain a sound no-faults container. One version of this container had a bark edge skirt, whose natural weathering and small cracks all added to the effect. A client who was a keen astronomer commissioned what became the final form. Later variations saw square, triangular and round clean skirts, however perfecting the spherical container section was the challenge and the determining factor in the overall success of each piece.

This project is not ideal for the novice, although I would like to think that attempting it would help many woodturners develop new skills. The stock chosen for the planet sphere needs to be a stable timber that holds together well in the heartwood and can ideally retain its bark around its waney edge. Camphor laurel, jacaranda, sandalwood, olive, Huon pine and many others are suitable (sandalwood is shown here). I recommend using dry timber, as shrinkage after turning can cause heartache when off-round lids and bases no longer fit together. Green timbers can be used if they are stable.

An increased success rate will come from keeping the centre of the heartwood as close to the centre of the turning as possible. This will normally even out the shrinkage around the lid and base section, although uneven growth rings will often prove this theory wrong. I must emphasise careful selection of the branch or trunk section

5

6

7

for your stock, as this will help prevent disappointment later. I've turned these forms from branches as narrow as 30mm and from trunk sections as wide as 350mm.

Cut your section clear of any deep cracks or knots that may run into the centre area where you will be shaping the sphere. Small cracks and knots around the outer edge are acceptable and can add character to the skirt edge. The length must make allowances for loss of timber in mounting between centres and in push fit chucks. The length of the blank should be approximately the same as its average width.

Mark a centre on each end of the blank. I generally like to keep the centre in the middle of the growth rings (heartwood) as this adds a nice symmetry to the spherical section. However nature is not always obliging and to avoid spinning the blank too off-centre a compromise will sometimes have to be made.

Mount the blank between centres (photo 1) and true the outer edges into a cylinder leaving a bark edge skirt (around 10mm thick) just above the halfway length of the blank (photo 2). To avoid catching your gouge and tearing off the bark edge, all cuts should be away from the skirt area and towards the centre. These will all be with the grain. Cut a 90° stepped flange on each end of the blank for mounting the base into a spigot or 4-jaw chuck, and for push fitting the lid into the base (photo 3). If you do not have a chuck the blank can be screwed directly onto a faceplate before turning.

If you are turning larger pieces make sure you use long screws to give good holding strength into the endgrain and you will need to leave an extra allowance of length for this. For small blanks (under 50mm) these 90° flanges can be turned to push fit into a waste block attached either to a chuck or faceplate.

After the flanges have been turned, check the cylinder is clean of any faults. Its diameter should be between a half to a third of the average diameter of the skirt area. At this stage, using a drawing compass, mark two semi-circular 'templates' on thin cardboard—one will be around 1mm smaller in diameter than the cylinder you have turned, the other will be 4-6mm smaller again. The larger template will be used to check the external shape of the sphere, the smaller for checking the internal profile of the lid and base. The difference in their size will determine the finished wall thickness of the sphere. Cut the templates out. Now you can start to shape the outside of the sphere up to where the flanges start. If you find this difficult to do by eye, use the template. Once you have the general shape, use very fine cuts to thin the skirt area back to 4-3mm, concaving the underside and curving the top side downward. (I recommend using a 1/2" spindle gouge shaped to a fine fingernail profile for this.)

A tip to help retain the thin bark edge is to run some thin cyanoacrylate glue into the area where the bark and sapwood join. Avoid water marks by quickly wiping the surface with a lint free cloth. When set (30-60 seconds), lightly sand and finish. This glue is also marvellous for hiding and strengthening fine heartwood cracks.

When shaping the lid it is important to make allowance for parting it off. I use an old power hacksaw blade I've shaped into a parting tool and set into a handle. These make ideal parting tools and minimise the loss of timber in the 1.5mm wide cut they produce.

With work still mounted between centres, part the lid almost off leaving a 10mm neck. Remove the work from between centres and mount it into your chuck. Completely part or cut the lid off.

Using vernier calipers, check the size of the flange of the lid (photo 4). With the calipers set at this size, rest the left tip on the internal gauge on the tool rest and very lightly bring it into contact with the spinning surface of the base section. By drawing the calipers slowly along the surface, a circle the exact size of the setting can be marked by sighting the right tip on the opposite side of the circle. I find this the most accurate way to size all my push fit flanges and steps (photo 5).

Note: only the left tip of the calipers should touch the spinning surface whilst being kept on the toolrest at all times. At no time bring the right tip into contact with the spinning surface otherwise it will be flicked up with ferocious speed—be careful!

The mark left by the calipers is then scraped out leaving a 90° step (photo 6). The flange on the lid is then push fitted into the base leaving the lid facing outwards (photo 7). This fit must be tight—a slightly loose fit can be made tighter by wetting the step and flange with water. Rough out the lid using a suitably sized deep fluted gouge until the lid is about 4mm thick (photo 8). Use the smaller semi-circular template to check the interior shape. The template should go in until it sits flush with the lid rim. Finish the inside with a round-nose scraper—keep these cuts light to avoid tearing out the endgrain. At the same time smooth off to the outside edge leaving the rim 2-3mm thick.

I normally start sanding with 120 grit and progress through 150, 180, 220, 280, 320, 400. A finish can now be applied to the inside of the lid. I often use grape seed oil as it is odourless and doesn't become rancid. In this way the natural scent of timbers such as camphor laurel, Huon pine and sandalwood is preserved and the wood will still have a silky finish.

Gently remove lid from the pushed fit, parting away the internal area of the base around the fitted area to release it if necessary.

Using the vernier calipers set them to the outside circumference of the lid (photo 9). Following the procedure outlined before, carefully mark this size onto the interior of the base. Scrape a step about 2-3mm deep and push fit the lid into the base. Bring the tail stock lightly into contact with the flange on top of the lid to prevent it pulling out. Using the larger outside template to check the shape of the lid, turn off the flange and waste wood (photo 10).

Sand and apply your finish. Be careful

not to undercut the rim of the lid which is protected by the step in the base. Remove the finished lid and rough out the base, scraping it smooth in the same way as for the inside of the lid—use the inside template to check its shape. Note that the half circle template should sit flush with the bottom edge of the step you turned into the base. When the lid is now fitted, a close to perfectly spherical interior will be formed if you have used the inside template accurately. Sand the interior of the base and the top side of skirt and apply your chosen finish. If you had a very tight fitting lid remove about 0.1mm from the step. Ideally the lid should glide into the base. Remember that heat from sanding friction can warp your lid and base. This will settle, so do not remove too much from the step.

Now cut waste away from the bottom area of the base. A critical area is where the corner of the lower side of skirt meets the spherical area. Be very careful not to cut this too thin, otherwise you will part the skirt through into the internal step. Either make the skirt slightly thicker here (say 4mm if step is 2-3mm) or round off the corner leaving the area where the skirt and lower part of the sphere meet, slightly thicker.

Part the base off leaving about 12mm of waste timber in the chuck. Turn a small bowl-like stand from this waste and hollow it underneath by push fitting it back into the remaining waste timber. This stand will be approximately one third of the sphere's diameter. The base can now be sanded and finished. Mount a scrap piece of timber into the lathe and use the vernier calipers again to mark this with the step size in the base. Turn a flange and push fit the base onto it bringing the tail stock centre lightly onto the underside of the base.

Turn the lower side of the base (photo 11) checking the shape with the outside template. Sand and finish the lower side of the skirt and base. If all has gone well you should have your very own planet sphere. I hope it inspires you to seek new frontiers and go where no man has gone... Good luck!

Totally Turned Tables

Turning furniture componentry is not new, yet both the top and legs of these attractive occasional tables were turned on the lathe. Andrew Potocnik demonstrates how.

Part of my work is creating components for other people's work, which, more often than not, are required for the making of furniture. Frequently, however, I am taken by the urge to create my own pieces of furniture. True to my passion, though, turning dominates and becomes the focal technique used.

Shortly after beginning work on a possible design I realised there was potential for a number of variations, two of which I made. One is a table of natural feature grade mountain ash with turned legs, the other, made of red gum, has a turned top and legs.

My focus here is on turning, rather than the joinery techniques involved in the making of these coffee tables. Without doubt there are alternative ways of executing the designs, these solutions are merely examples.

'Stiletto Table I'

Three boards of natural feature grade mountain ash were machined to size, glued together and sash clamped for the top (photo 1). I drew lines radiating from the centre to help with the marking out of the shape and later on these were essential for determining the placement of the three legs. The top was then cut and sanded accordingly (photo 2).

Knowing the standard height of a coffee table to be in the vicinity of 450mm, I used any object available to raise the top to that height (photo 3) so that I could gauge the required length and diameter of the legs. Proportions were thus established by eye, keeping in mind restrictions imposed by existing stock sizes.

Once the timber for the legs was cut and mounted on the lathe, the form was rough-turned to near final diameter, and the length from toe to shoulder marked and a round tenon (or spigot) was turned. I find this process easiest to complete with a parting tool (photo 4). Dimensions were checked with vernier calipers (photo 5). The remainder of the leg was turned to shape and size, then sanded. Photo 6 shows the three legs completed.

There are a number of ways of attaching the legs to the

table top. You need to consider the strength—for example, is a frame or reinforcement required? Do you anticipate the top will move due to air moisture changes, or will the timber cup on account of being back-sawn? Is the top too thin for its size to carry substantial weight? These are a few of the factors influencing the nature of the final structure. Wanting my table to be simple in design and construction, I chose to join the legs directly into the top, hence the tenons on each leg.

There are a couple of choices available. One method is to fit the tenon into a block which is then screwed underneath the top (photo 7). To strengthen the joint between the leg and block, cut a slot in the top of the tenon and insert a wedge (photo 8)—this flares the tenon to increase its grip in the block. Thinking laterally, the legs could also be angled into the block, giving the table another kind of balance and style. Another way would be to drill a hole directly through the top, making a feature of the exposed endgrain (photo 9).

'Stiletto' Table II

In essence, this table is the same as the one described so far, however this time I relied even more on turning rather than joinery, choosing to turn the underneath of the top as well as the legs.

Once the redgum had been machined and joined for the top it was mounted on the lathe, enabling me to turn the underside. I wanted a gentle flowing curve graduating from a thicker centre to thinner edges. This would produce an interesting effect once cut to a three-sided form. To prove that the table top was turned, I cut some circular lines in the centre of the top surface (photo 10). To add more interest, I bevelled underneath the top making the exposed edge thickness vary from corner to middle of each of the three curved sides (photo 11).

Joining legs vertically into a curved form presented me with a couple of problems, foremost being how to join a straight shoulder into a curved surface. The simplest solution I felt would be to create a rebated surface for the leg's shoulder to fit into. To achieve this I used a hole saw and chisel to produce the rebated hole with a round shoulder and flat face (photo 12). A Forstner bit would have been very handy at this point! For this step to be successful, it was imperative to line up centres of rebate and tenon holes.

Later I developed a variety of possible methods with which these designs could be developed further, especially in splaying turned legs when joined into a flat top, or joining splayed legs into a curved surface. It has probably been done hundreds of times in the last few thousand years, however nothing can take away the joy of 'discovering' a solution to a design problem!

You can't, however, lose sight of the balance needed between innovative design and what a sometimes conservative market is willing to tolerate. If you're trying to make a living from your work it is futile to create objects which don't have a market, regardless of how 'different' or 'interesting' they are.

These tables rely on a combination of clean, uncluttered lines and simple construction techniques. An exposed through tenon reduces the need for substantial frames, skirts and other supporting structures often associated with table construction. The result is an easy to construct table with few visible structural components.

Although traditional makers may well see structural problems associated with these designs, my intention was to confront conventional constructional techniques and explore conceptual and visual potential in the application of turned components to furniture.

Purse Mirrors

These small hand held purse mirrors are an ideal production item, and here Terry Martin shows how to streamline the process of making them.

The average hobby turner is happy to make a small number of pieces and give them to friends and relatives, or keep them as special mementos. Some are tempted to try selling their work on a larger scale, but the realities of marketing and production frequently put them off. Nevertheless, it is possible to make a profit from a home workshop if you have a simple, marketable product and are prepared to invest a little time and money to become efficient. This project shows how to make one such product—a purse mirror.

I have chosen the mirror for this project because it is small enough to be made on almost any lathe. It uses very little timber and is a high value-added product which can give a reasonable return on outlay and time. My first attempts at these mirrors were woefully inefficient. Each mirror probably took me half an hour as I fiddled with chucking arrangements and, years later, I work on a maximum turning time of five minutes per mirror, although with good wood I can turn one every three minutes. This is a bit of an illusion as it does not include all the other stages of production, such as blank-cutting, storage, sorting, polishing and gluing in the mirrors. This increase in speed has been achieved by reducing the number of steps and tools used and, where possible, combining two or three movements into one single step.

Although it could be done with other chucks I think it is best to use a scroll chuck for this process, to save changing jaws, but it is easy to do the same work with one chuck. You need jaws large enough to mount the blank for initial cutting and small jaws for reverse-chucking. Both the large and small *Vicmarc* chucks are suitable, as is the *Teknatool Nova* chuck. I use one tailor-made cutter which I ground myself, but the other tools are usually owned by every hobby turner.

The starting point is the mirror itself. There are various sizes available, but I prefer the 63.5mm wide size. I cut the wood blanks 85mm square and about 15mm thick on my bandsaw. Originally I started turning mirrors because I didn't want to throw away off-cuts, especially when I had bought the wood. In the first flush of enthusiastic recycling I turned mirrors out of almost every off-cut. I soon learnt the public don't buy a mirror because it is an efficient use of resources—they want a mirror that features attractive wood grain. Now I select and cut the pieces with this in mind. After cutting blanks I store them for some time to dry, ensuring maximum air circulation.

Before I start a run of mirrors, I organise everything so I can work smoothly. I have a small table which sits at the height of my lathe bed. It has small strips of wood nailed to three sides, so when I lay a tool down it can't roll off. On the table I lay out the gouges (one deep-fluted for rough cuts and two detail gouges), sandpaper, sanding pad and chuck levers. I keep two boxes beside the lathe. Box one contains unturned blanks. After the first side is done, the blanks are placed in box two, ready for reverse chucking. They go back to box one when they are finished.

First I mount the blank in the *Nova* chuck using the 80mm accessory jaws. I don't cut the blanks round on the bandsaw because it is quicker on the lathe. I then take off the front of the corners with the deep-fluted gouge, taking care not to cut into the jaws. For maximum control I pivot the gouge over the toolrest, rolling it into the work like a see-saw (photo 1). I could use one gouge for the whole process, but I prefer to keep the detail gouges sharp for the finishing cuts. Next I need to cut one recess for the mirror and another small recess for rechucking to turn the other side.

The larger recess needs to be 64mm wide and the smaller one has to be slightly larger than the jaws used to rechuck the piece—in my case 32mm for the long-nosed *Vicmarc* jaws. It is possible to cut the recesses separately using two saw-tooth or Forstner bits, but they are expensive and time consuming to use as it is necessary to remount each bit in the tailstock for each cut. Another way is to mark out the recesses with dividers or a tailor-made marking gauge and then cut them using scrapers.

I have saved most time in this process by grinding my own cutter (photo 2). I have cut marks every 5mm in the

1

2

3

tailstock quill and I simply read it off as I wind in (these marks are also very useful when boring out other jobs to a specific depth, such as hollowing boxes). For most woods it isn't necessary to reduce speed. The flat cutter is so quick the wood doesn't have time to heat up. If I am using a very hard wood, such as one of the acacias, I may reduce speed. I use a *Vicmarc* mechanical variable speed lathe, so I don't have to stop the lathe to change speed. Any of the electronic variable speed lathes would also do the job.

Next I use a detail gouge (3/8" spindle gouge) to cut the rim of the mirror in three steps. First I cut inwards to shape the outer rim (photo 3). This is a light cut, as pushing too hard would tear off wood from the edge of the recess. I need to end up with a recess slightly deeper than the 2mm thick mirror. I find 3mm deep about right.

Then I finish the inside of the recess. This is only to dress the rough cut left by the cutter, so the minimum of wood is removed. I use the point of the gouge and brace my hand against kickback (photo 4—glove off for clarity).

The third cut is a pulled shear-scrape using the edge of the gouge which is rolled over on its side so the flute is towards me. This cut cleans up the rim and gives me a better finish. If you are uncertain about the size of the recess, you can check it by inserting a mirror. It should have enough room around it to allow for expansion and contraction of the wood under different conditions (approximately 0.5mm all round). I have a mirror mounted on a rubber suction cup, which makes handling and removal easier.

Now I am ready for sanding. Without turning off, I again slide the toolrest away and start with the finest paper I can. Assuming I have got the best cut possible in the previous step, it will depend entirely on the wood I am using. With the camphor laurel I am using in the photo I can usually start at 150 grit and work through 180, 240 and 320. On some timbers such as ebony, I go as fine as 600 grit.

Any of the better brands of cloth-backed abrasive will do. Cheap

4

abrasives are false economy as they shed grit into the work, wear out quickly and end up costing more in time and money. I back the abrasive with a pad of leather, which both insulates my fingers and absorbs heat from the wood, reducing the chance of cracking. I brace my right hand with my left to control pressure (photo 5). If you have to push too hard, the abrasive is not cutting. Clogged paper can be cleared with a brisk rap on the bed of the lathe, but using worn paper is inefficient and will overheat the work.

After I have finished all of the mirror fronts I change chucks. Generally I will do a run of 50-100 mirrors in a session. If you are using one chuck, this is the time to change to the smaller jaws. I use the *Vicmarc* long-nosed jaws because I can sand right around the rim without catching my fingers. However, this will leave less room around the rim for sanding and the chance of cracking is greater because this is the thinnest part of the blank. The blank is remounted by expanding the jaws into the inner recess (photo 6). Don't overdo it—experience will show how hard to open the jaws.

The square corners are cut off with the same rolling action used in stage one. It is important not to push too hard into the wood, as the rim has less support than before. Let the lathe do the work, which is probably a good rule at any time. Then I rough the back with the deep-fluted gouge. From now on all

5

6

7

8

cuts should be outwards to the rim as the fibres are supported in that direction, just as when you cut the bottom of a bowl from the base to the rim.

Too much pressure or removal of too much wood will break off the rim. Practice will show how thin to go, but less than 2mm is risky. I then finish-cut with the detail gouge (photo 7). To achieve the best shape I lean over the work, looking down so I can see both the curve I am cutting and how thin the piece is.

Finish sanding is done with the same sequence of grits. I use the first grit to round over the rim and blend in with the other side. Again, don't push too hard here or you will snap off the rim. A final rub along the grain with the lathe switched off will eliminate any fine scratches (photo 8).

My special cutter is a reground *Woodfast Superchuck* cutter. First I ground the ends so that it was 64mm wide and then I ground the stepped front bevels. Mark the widths with a scriber and take light cuts towards the end for accuracy. Cool the cutter frequently in water while grinding.

I cut a small dovetail in the end of the long-nosed jaws with a scraper. The jaws are quite soft and will accept this cut at slow speed if they are fully closed. The recess can only be cut straight-sided with the cutter and the dovetail seats more positively and gives a firmer grip.

I oil my mirrors with two coats of *Penetrol*. Other finishes such as Danish oil will do, but don't use wax as it will not stand up to the rigours of rattling around in a purse. I attach the mirrors to the wood with a thin bead of silicon gum—I line up the mirrors on a bench and apply it to them all in one operation. The mirrors can be pressed down on the silicon and located in the centre of the blank (photo 9). After they are set, a quick wipe with turps will remove fingermarks and silicon spills.

If you really want to go up-market you can make small bags for the purses. It increases their saleability and makes point-of-sale packaging easier. A small drawstring bag or a simple flap closure words well. They can be made from cloth or soft leather.

This product is a value-added item which uses very small amounts of wood for maximum return. It is suited to turners who can't or don't want to turn large pieces. You can use almost any stable timber, including garden waste and offcuts from other turning. It also allows you to practise basic techniques which are applicable to other jobs, such a bowl turning.

Pricing is up to you, but keep in mind there are turners out there paying the bills from their work. It is hard for them to appreciate competition from others who just cover the cost of their sandpaper. Be realistic and add up all of your costs, including your own labour.

9

Kitchen Spatulas

Richard Raffan shows how to turn your workshop off-cuts into attractive and functional kitchen spatulas.

Every woodworker has short lengths of scrap wood which look as though they might be good for something other than a fireplace...one day. Most of us allow these to accumulate in racks or bins only to gather dust whilst waiting for their time to come. Wedge-shaped off-cuts can be easily made into excellent kitchen spatulas which are ideal for use in non-stick pans and, being wood, are much more appealing than their plastic cousins.

In demonstrations and workshops over the years, I've suggested to many cash-strapped individuals that spatulas would be a useful way of transforming their straight-grained waste into cash whilst providing kitchen and craft shops with the sort of small item they cry out for. Several people have gone on to develop businesses which make very little else.

Off-cuts can be roughly shaped on a bandsaw, then completed using disc or belt sanders. But if you have a lathe it's possible to incorporate turned elements whilst getting some excellent practice for the skew chisel. The spatula in this exercise consists of a skewed blade which flows into a 13mm (1/2") shaft and on to a slightly fatter rounded handle. The slight curve of the shaft looks best if it flows smoothly beneath the decorative bead.

I cut blanks on a bandsaw into a vague wedge, with a wide but thin blade at one end and a section 20-30mm (3/4" to 1- 3/16") square at the other for the handle. If I want a curved blade the blank will be thicker at the blade end.

If you want to create a particular shape, draw the outline on one face of the blank as in photo 1. You'll see the line as the wood spins on the lathe and can cut to that.

I like to have the blade to the left so that if necessary I can stop the lathe and test the feel of the handle with my right hand. When working this way around between centres you need a suitably small spur drive no wider than the end of the blade. The end-grain will be damaged, although this is not a problem since this portion is usually cut away in the final shaping when the end is skewed to make the spatula easier to use. If you have only a standard spur drive of 25mm (1"), you'll need to have the handle towards the headstock where there is more wood for the spurs to grip. A good alternative and more secure grip is to mount the blade end in a chuck as in photo 2, especially if you want to set the blade off-centre for an asymmetric form.

Initial shaping and roughing down is easiest using a centre work roughing gouge starting at the end of the blank, photo 3. Have the gouge flute facing the end of the blank as you take a series of scooping cuts, first to make the handle round, then develop the profile of the blade. Next pivot the skew chisel long point into the wood about 6mm (3/16") at 90° to the axis to define the blade side of the bead (photo 4). By cutting across the fibres you ensure a clean termination to the finishing shear cuts which follow.

Turn the blade and shank using a 19mm (3/4") skew chisel (photo 5). This is wonderful skew chisel practice and I use a slightly radiused oval skew whose bevel shoulder is less likely to mark the wood as I cut the long concave curve between the blade and shank. With only a narrow section of wood spinning past the edge, if you push too hard it's easy to take the tool into the gap and have a catch. The secret to obtaining a smooth surface off the tool, as with all woodturning, is to let the wood come to the tool, then keep the bevel rubbing the wood when (in this case) there is wood to rub. Cut using the leading and lower half of

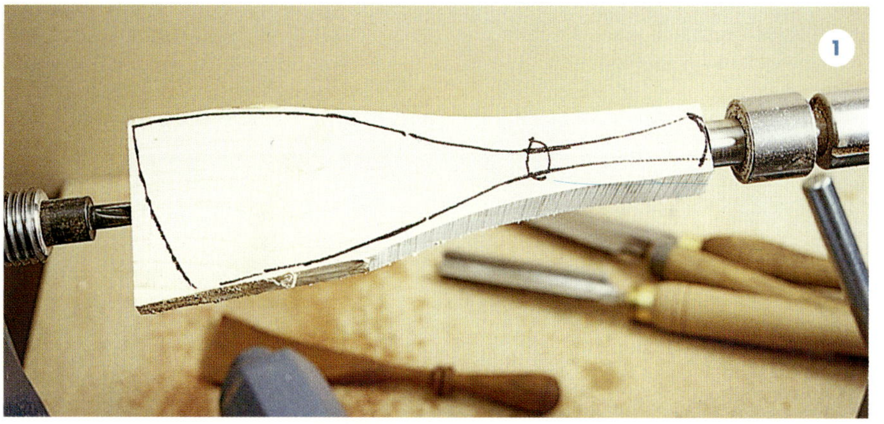

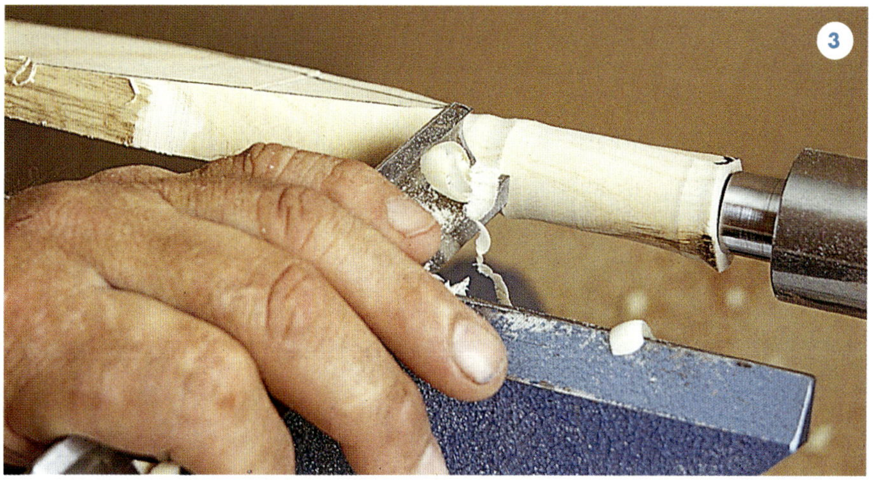

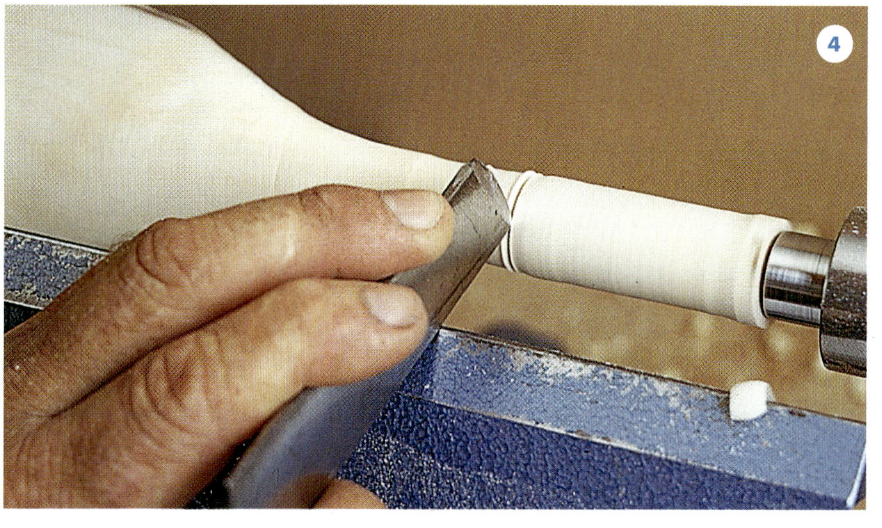

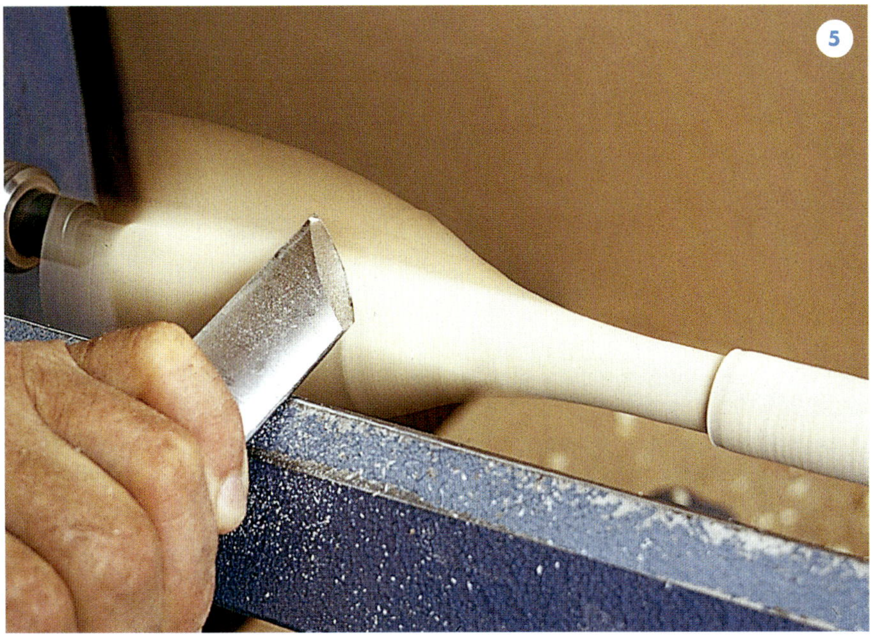
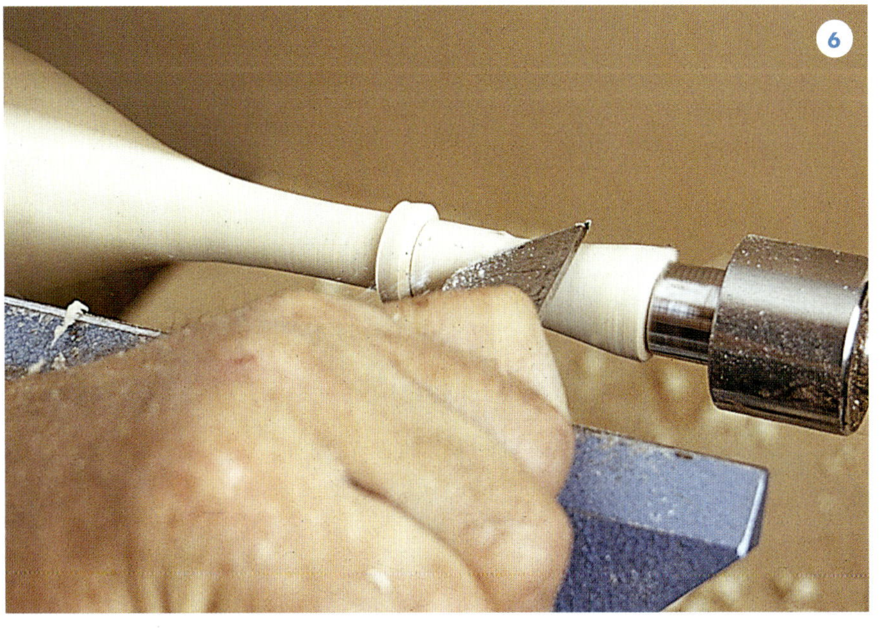

the edge, easing the handle around so that you use the corner of the tool to cut into the base of the bead. If you get a frill of material at the base of the bead, you'll need to take another light cut at 90° to the axis using the skew long point. In this situation I favour a standard rectangular section skew chisel which has a longer bevel side than the oval tool. Then, using the long point only, the point and bevel side are in contact with the wood.

Use the same skew chisel to take another 90° cut to define the handle side of the bead before shaping the handle as in photo 6. Turn the shaft so it flows smoothly beneath the roughed bead. Then complete the bead and turn the end of the handle leaving just enough material to support the job (photo 7). Try to avoid pointy ends on the handle: you often want to use a spatula with the end against your palm, and it will be much more comfortable if rounded If you're having trouble turning rounded beads, go for squarer forms of decoration until your confidence grows.

With the turning completed, sand the spatula with the abrasive folded in three as in photo 8. The blade will want to slap your fingers around, so hold the abrasive at either end to keep your fingers clear. If you cut the wood cleanly, you should be able to start using 120 grit, followed by 180 and 240 grit and then finer as desired. I apply an oil finish off the lathe when all the final shaping and sanding is completed.

Once you've finished, part the spatula free at the handle end using the long point of a skew chisel, as in photo 9. If you keep your thumb on the rest it acts as a fulcrum, but, more usefully, it prevents the handle hitting the rest (sustaining damage) in the parting-off process.

When refining the shape of the spatula blade I remove larger amounts of waste using a bandsaw before moving to the belt sander (photos 10 and 11). Cut the skewed end last in order to lessen the risk of the spatula being grabbed by the saw.

For final shaping of the blade I go to a sander with a 100 grit belt, or 60

grit if there is a lot of material to remove (photo 12). The long corner of any spatula intended for use in a saucepan needs to be slightly less than 90° so that it reaches right into the corner of the pan. Wok stirrers are best with radiused ends so they fit to the curve of a wok.

For final sanding, I find a lathe mounted 75mm (3") soft sanding pad with velcro-backed discs mounted in a chuck on the lathe most convenient. Popping discs on and off in a few seconds beats changing belts on the sander.

When sanding is completed, I finish the spatulas with mineral or cooking oil. To maintain these useful tools once they're in use, simply hand wash in hot water and detergent. Spatulas in constant use become even smoother with use and do not require further oiling.

The variety of forms you can create is almost limitless and the principles can be adapted to making paper knives, butter spreaders or, with a deeper blade section and a bit more carving, spoons. By off-setting the blank, you can turn one side of an asymmetric blade, leaving the other to be shaped on the bandsaw and sander. And may this help to reduce your off-cuts.

Making Pens

A turned pen is an ideal gift or souvenir item, especially when made from highly figured or exotic timbers. Inexpensive to make in terms of materials, your own skill and design sense will add value proportionately. Gary Beck shows you how to turn a pen step by step.

Since their introduction to Australia, pen movements, which accept custom-turned timber blanks, have been sold literally by the thousand, and although not the very latest thing, continue to sell well. The pens produced look and feel good and make a readily acceptable gift. A small initial outlay will equip you with the specialty chucks and mandrels needed to turn pens in volume, whilst the pen movements themselves are also inexpensive.

Wooden pens consist of a shop bought pen movement, which is fitted into a drilled hollow timber cylinder with a turned outside surface. Virtually any timber is suitable for pens, but it must be dry. As you are using tiny amounts of timber, pens are an ideal opportunity to use some of the world's most exotic and precious woods for a low cost.

Timber blanks should be sawn to around 12-14mm square (most woodturning suppliers sell pen blanks in exotic timbers, half inch square and in long lengths). Cut the blank, around 2mm longer than the brass tubes for the movement. In photo 1, I have used the brass tube as a length measuring guide while cutting on the bandsaw.

Using a straight sharp drill bit (dowelling bits are preferred), drill a 7mm hole in the blank by either mounting the blank in a vice and using a drill press, or by mounting the blank in a chuck and using the tailstock with a drill chuck (photo 2).

Drilling in the lathe is more accurate but slower. Glue the two brass tubes,

1

2

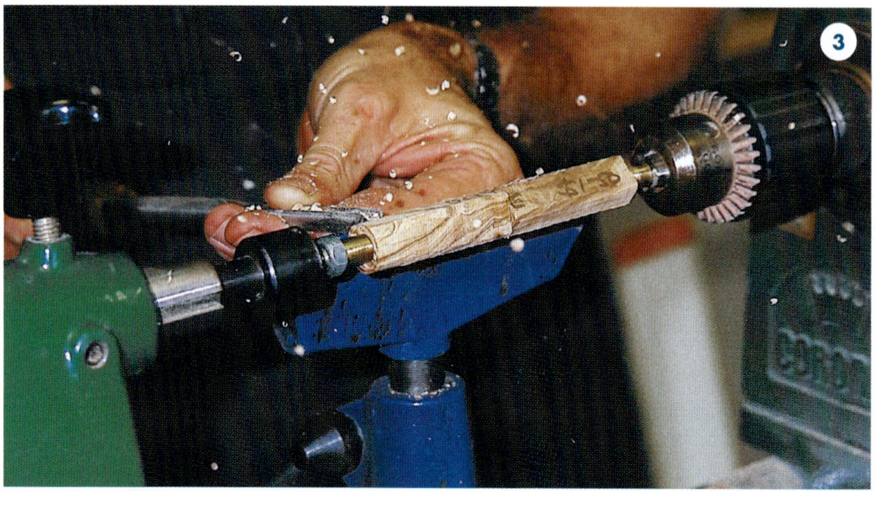

3

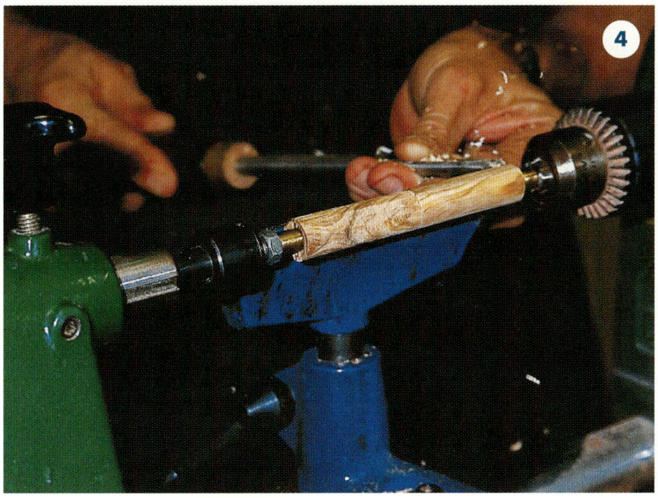

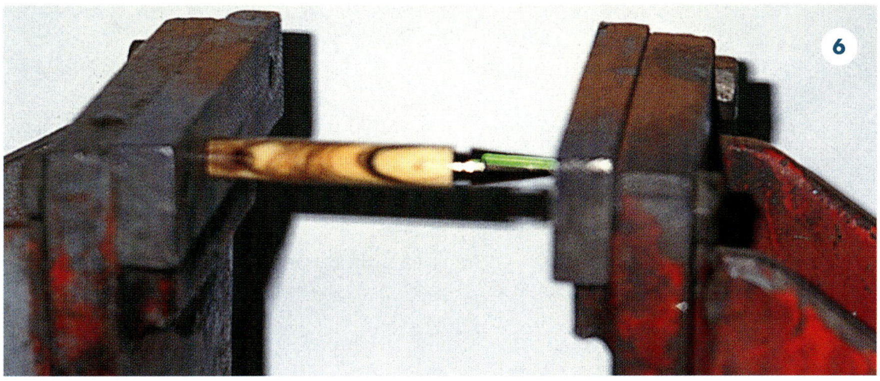

one inside in each blank. A cyanoacrylate such as *Superglue* works well, however epoxy or similar is acceptable. Let the glue set before squaring the timber off flush to the brass with a file, sander or pen mill. Pen mills are specially designed for this process and sold by specialist tool outlets. It is important that this squaring off is done with great accuracy. The blanks are then slid onto a mandrel which is a turning accessory specifically designed for pen making, and once again sold through retail outlets. You can make your own mandrel, however at a minimal cost they are a worthwhile purchase.

Mount the blanks and the mandrel in the lathe, being careful to maintain the grain orientation. The best way to secure the mandrel is with a drill chuck (photo 3). If you don't want to buy a mandrel and drill chuck you can turn the blanks by between centres mounting, however if the blanks aren't turned as one unit they may not be as accurately matched.

Turn the blanks down to the desired diameter, the brass end stops on the mandrel are a good guide for diameter size as this is the same diameter as pen mechanisms (photo 4). Best results are achieved using a skew chisel or gouge (beginners can use a scraper). Sand the blank to around 400 grit, however if you are using a mandrel take care not to sand into the brass end stops (photo 5). Apply a finish to the pen; I prefer a nitrocellulose lacquer, but oil or wax is fine.

Remove the pen blanks from the mandrel and you are now ready for final assembly. Taking care that grain orientation is always correct, use a vice and press fit the movements into place. Photo 6 shows how the tip is pressed first, then the inner mechanism as far as the indent mark in the same tube. Next slip the ring over the mechanism (brass top first) and screw in the refill. Press the cap through the clip and into the top assembly. Push the two halves together and you should now have a well balanced object which is a pleasure to hold and use.

Apart from the specific set up purchases of a drill chuck and a turning mandrel, your only other costs in turning pens will be for timber and sandpaper, both of which are used minimally. The cost of pen blanks will vary from nothing for offcuts, to a few dollars per pen for exotics such as purple heart, ebony and burl, or you can try alternatives such as laminated veneers, blocks of crushed velvet and tagua nuts.

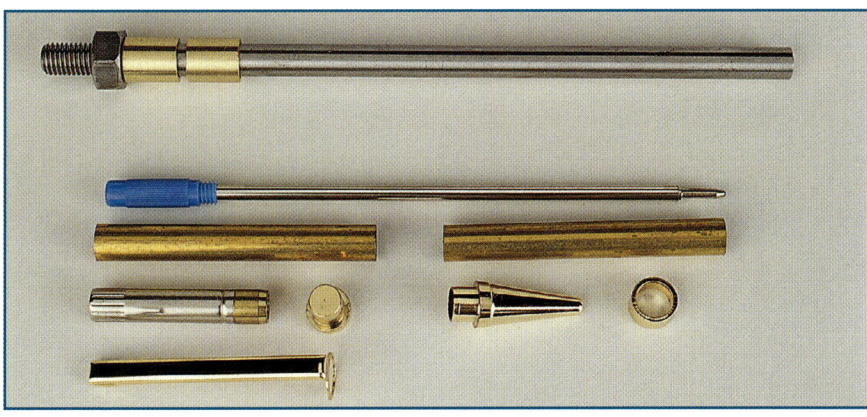

Tool Kit

To turn pens, you will need the following:

- Timber blank
- Mandrel (pictured left at the top)
- Pen movement (pictured left)
- Drill chuck
- Either drill press or scroll chuck for drilling
- Small gouge or skew chisel

Chopsticks and Presentation Box

Inspired by the natural segmentation of bamboo, Andrew Potocnik turns a cylinder flared at each end and halves it to form a presentation case for a set of chopsticks. Contrasting timbers and simple details create an elegant gift.

In my opinion, the simplest box that nature ever created is a neatly jointed cylinder of bamboo. In fact this shape inspired me to turn an elongated form that could both enclose and present an object. I chose to make my box for chopsticks, and this is how I made them.

Chopsticks

Select a timber that doesn't have any known toxic properties. I used some red gum which was free of figure and unusual grain. Experience has taught me that it is very difficult to turn long thin pieces if the grain isn't clear and straight. Remember to cut your timber a little oversize so that you can plane it to size later on. Only the handle will remain square, and this needs to be planed neatly, free of saw marks and tears. You can also use a disc sander, belt sander or linisher to dress the wood. If you don't have a sander you can easily make a disc and table that can be fitted to a lathe (photo 1), assuming that you have one of those!

If all has gone according to plan, you should soon have two pieces of wood about 7mm x 7mm x 250mm long that are ready to shape. These measurements can be altered to suit. I shaped the round tapered section of each stick on the lathe, but you can also achieve good results by planing, sanding, spokeshaving or filing them.

If you are turning them, it is possible to hold the wood between centres, but be sure not to over-tighten your quill, or the wood will bow. Support the wood while turning as it is quite flexible (photo 2). Rest your forearm on the headstock, curl your fingers under the work, resting them on the underneath part of the toolrest, and gently press the middle part of your fingers against the spinning wood. Be sure to use very sharp tools and cut gently,

twenty at a Chinese grocery store. At this rate you could find yourself working for a couple of cents per hour!

Once the sticks were completed, I felt that it would be nice to add contrasting timber to the end of each stick to add a little interest. For this I chose rock maple, the same timber used for the box. Photo 4 shows square lines marked on the parts of each piece of wood that would be joined. I sanded these surfaces square and flat on the disc sander. The rock maple sections were left about 1mm wider and thicker than required so they would be easy to trim to size.

You can use a dowel to join the stick and the end, or (as there isn't a lot of stress on this joint) simply glue the two pieces together. I used a long lasting, water resistant glue (*Araldite* two-part epoxy resin). After gluing, clamp the two pieces and set them aside to dry.

Next, plane the rock maple to the same size as the red gum. I used a simple planing block to hold the wood so that I could work freely. You could also use a disc sander or a sanding board for this. (To make a sanding board, simply attach a sheet of abrasive paper to a flat board using staples or glue. This board enables you to sand objects flat and smooth, and when clamped to the bench, frees both hands.) Sand each of the sides through to their finished state (320 grit or higher), sanding with the grain to minimise scratches. Next, cut the eating end of the chopsticks off straight. I used a fine-toothed fret saw in order to reduce the chipping of fibres. To create a slightly different appearance on the maple ends, I cut each end diagonally to create a diamond shape when viewed end-on.

Sand the ends prior to finishing. Cooking oil is the most appropriate finish in this case, but be careful to select one that doesn't become rancid. Canola oil is suitable, so wipe it on liberally, allow it to soak in, then wipe off the excess and leave to dry.

Presentation Box

Cut a suitable piece (300mm x 50mm x 50mm) of rock maple in half lengthwise, plane the two cut surfaces flat and PVA them back together with a sheet of paper in between (photo 5). Laminating the paper allows you to separate the two halves for the top and bottom of the box. Rather than trying to cut the sleeve in half later, it is much easier to split the paper joint. The separated surfaces require only minimal cleaning and the result is a fully rounded cylinder, not two near halves. Take care to plane the surfaces as flat as possible, otherwise if you have gaps, the wood can de-laminate while turning. Obviously this could be extremely dangerous, not to mention frustrating if you need to start again.

Before beginning on my rock maple, I turned a test piece from a scrap of radiata pine to see if my intended form and dimensions were correct. This also helped to predict any problems that might arise.

the wood is flexible and prone to breakage. If you're planing or filing your chopsticks, mark out sections where the taper will start, then clamp the wood to a supporting block held in a vice. Plane or file one corner at a time, gradually working down to a circular taper. If planing, hold your plane on an angle to the wood so that the blade slices the fibres to leave a smooth surface (photo 3).

If you're thinking of mass producing chopsticks, then you may wish to do all the shaping on a disc sander, but be realistic if you hope to sell them. I recently paid $1.20 for a packet of

When mounting the block between centres, line up the lathe's centres with the glue line in your timber to guarantee two perfect halves. Rough turn your block into a cylinder, then turn each end down to 60mm diameter. I used vernier calipers to measure the diameters. In photo 6 the glue joint is visible at 'eleven o'clock'.

Turn the cylinder to shape, retaining the 60mm ends and working down to 43mm diameter at the thinnest point halfway along (photo 7). Remove the bulk of material with a roughing gouge, then use a scraper to refine the form. Check the form by eye to see that the left and right halves are even, or use a profile gauge.

Once the form is perfect, sand through 120, 240, 320 and 400 grit abrasives. Finish off by hand sanding with the grain. Don't over-sand or you'll lose definition of the form.

Next, mount the wood in some form of holding device, so that one end is left free, enabling you to hollow out the inside of the box. I made a carrier from scrap timber and screwed it to the faceplate. Into this I cut a hole or rebate identical to the diameter of the rock maple and about 6-7mm deep. Note in photo 8 how the extra hole in the centre has been cut to accommodate the stub left at one end of the wood which will be needed later.

Glue the rock maple with PVA into the carrier, push the centre of the tailstock back to where it was when you were turning the outside. Tighten it to hold the wood centred and clamped at the same time (photo 9) and leave to dry overnight. The wood should run true once the tailstock is removed.

Once dry, fit a Jacob's-type chuck to

the tailstock, insert the largest diameter drill bit you have and drill as far into the blank as possible, preferably more than halfway so the other end can be drilled out later. I used a spade bit as it cuts quickly and easily.

Once drilled, the hole can be enlarged and shaped to correspond to the outside form. One way of removing waste from the inside is to insert a scraper about 10mm into the hole and scrape towards you along the grain. Scraping into endgrain requires a lot more pressure. Experiment with different scrapers and techniques to see which suits your style and level of ability.

An alternative way of clearing the waste is to use a small gouge and carefully work your way into the end grain of the wood. At the centre the gouge is rolled over and used to cut upside down, coming out on the reverse side. Remember to practise new techniques first.

Once I got to the stage of hollowing out deep into the cylinder, I changed over to a *Stewart System* shear scraper, which I found ideal. Use calipers to check for even wall thickness.

I used a piece of dowelling wrapped with abrasive paper (attached with masking tape) to sand the inside. When sanding, support the cylinder with your other hand to counter any pressure. Be very careful when inserting the sanding rod into the cylinder as it is very easy to lose control and hurt yourself.

Reverse the cylinder and repeat the full process. Before removing the cylinder

from its carrier, I cut two decorative V-grooves at each end with the long point of the skew. To support the wood, I first turned a plug out of some scrap timber, then held it in place with the tailstock (photo 10). This needs to be done after sanding has been completed so the line stays sharp.

Split the completed cylinder in half along the paper line by gently easing a sharp knife into the paper and slowly pushing it along, separating the paper as you go. Scrape the separated surfaces clean. Sand the two surfaces flat and smooth using a sanding board, again working through various grades of abrasive. Any visible cross grain scratches on the inside will now need to be removed by hand sanding along the grain.

The red gum supports were measured, cut, shaped and glued into position (photo 11). Shaping to final form was done on the disc sander by constant testing. Notches were cut and filed to position the chopsticks. Once complete, the supports were glued into position, after pre-finishing with polyurethane.

The stands were also made of red gum which was cut and shaped in the same way as the supports, then sanded through to 400 grit and finished. To sand and shape the concave surfaces I used a simple home-made device similar to a drum sander which is held between centres on the lathe.

Before attaching the stand to the box, I carefully marked where the four locating pins which hold the lid in place would go. These pins, or tiny spikes protrude from the surface of the lid and fit into corresponding holes in the lower half of the box. The spikes, turned in a Jacob's chuck, were 3mm long, 2mm diameter and had a 1.5mm tenon which fitted into holes that were drilled into the lid.

Once the spikes were completed and glued into position (photo 12) an oil-based satin polyurethane was applied liberally with a cloth and allowed to soak in for a few minutes. All the excess was wiped off with a dry cloth to leave a smooth surface. Finally, the supports were glued on and the finished product assembled.

Natural Edged Hollow Forms

Terry Martin shows how to turn a hollow form and preserve its natural edge.

A trained designer will plan a piece before approaching the lathe, though often, with a medium such as timber, Stephen Hughes admits 'nature will have the final say'[1]. Perhaps because I am not a trained designer, or maybe because of a different personality, I usually react to the wood and design as I go, incorporating the faults into the design.

With this in mind, I cut a wood blank from a fairly balanced log with the pith roughly in the same part of each end. The piece needs to be about as long as it is wide. I have chosen red cedar (*Toona australis*) because it is easily hollowed and stable. The timber is also slightly wet, which makes hollowing a lot easier.

With a piece of chalk I draw a line through the pith, dividing the end of the wood into two symmetrical halves (photo 1). I do the same at the other end and then join the lines along the length of the wood. Bisecting these lines half way along the length of the piece, mark the points for mounting the work between centres. I don't yet punch holes, or use any of the other traditional ways of ensuring a good bite for the drive dogs, because I may want to move these centres later.

Then I lightly mount the piece between centre, only bringing up the tailstock firmly enough to prevent the wood falling out. I place the toolrest near the work and line up another chalk mark on the rest with the pith at one end (photo 2). I then rotate the piece by hand to check how the pith on the other side lines up. If it is out of line, I back off the tailstock slightly and move the centre until I find the point where the pith at both ends is in line.

This is for two reasons. Firstly, it is aesthetically pleasing if they are balanced. Secondly, the wood will move after hollowing, either because of drying out, or release of the tensions. If the pith is aligned, the movement will be uniform and the piece will not lean to one side. Having found the position for that axis, I then address the position of the natural edge which will form the rim of the vessel. If I want a symmetrical rim, I move the opposite axes until I have achieved the degree of offset required.

Making sure the lathe is set at its lowest speed and that the toolrest is clear, I then start roughing to round, working from the low point 'uphill' to the centre (photo 3). At this stage the final parameters of the natural rim are set, although there is still room for minor adjustment. I keep roughing to round, gradually increasing the speed of the lathe as the piece be comes more balanced. I use a *Vicmarc* variable-speed lathe and at times like this I realise how convenient variable speed is. I can creep up to the maximum the piece will allow, with no fear of selecting the wrong speed.

When the piece is roughed I step back and gauge the final shape of the piece

by eye. This is a matter of compromise between the original dimensions of the wood, the practical need to turn a spigot on the foot, and the dimensions of the rim. I prefer very simple lines and try to achieve a small foot which lifts the work off the surface and gives an air of lightness to the piece. In this case I opted for an ovoid shape which narrowed more at the top than the bottom. I turn a spigot for remounting and then start refining the shape (photo 4). This stage is best done before remounting in the chuck as I have free acces to the very base of the piece, both for cutting and sanding.

For this type of work I use a *Henry Taylor HS24* gouge, or inch-and-a-quarter forged spindle gouge. I call it my 'big, flat gouge' and I often get very strange looks when people see me using it on bowls. The reason for using it is that I want to present the most open flute possible to the work. I find the shavings clear very cleanly and I am able to present the edge at a very flat angle. I suppose it is to bowl gouges what the skew is to spindle gouges. Cedar can be very 'picky' when cutting against the grain, as is necessary at some point in all vessel turning. I present the gouge very flat with the handle well down and take smooth, light pull-cuts uphill towards the centre.

When I am happy with the shape, I start sanding with velcro-backed sandpaper mounted on an arbor in an angle drill and work right to the base. Starting with 120 grit, I work up to about 180 and then examine the piece for faults that may crack if the piece shrinks. Here there are a few cracks, so I fill them with sawdust from the bed of the lathe. I then take a piece of the discarded sandpaper and soad a corner of the velcro in *Superglue*. This is then applied to the sawdust-filled cracks where it rapidly soaks in (photo 5).

This method saves glue and time. If you pour glue onto the cracks it easily runs down the surface of the piece, wasting glue and marring the already-sanded surface. By dabbing with the velcro, you have complete control over the quantity and location of application. I then finish sanding, in the case of cedar, all the way to 600 grit.

When the outside is satisfactorily finished, I can remount the piece in a chuck for hollowing (photo 6). Here I have chosen to start hollowing with a 3" saw-tooth bit, as it fits inside the dimensions of my natural rim. I mount the bit in a Jacob's chuck and set the lathe at its lowest speed. With a soft wood like cedar the heart can be bored out of the piece in a fraction of the time it takes to turn it. Be careful to check your depth before you start and, when you have checked it, check it again!

Then I start hollowing by using a deep-fluted gouge to quickly remove as much of the material as I can. I switch to the *Stewart System* cranked hollowing tool for the final internal cuts. Photo 7 is a turner's-eye view along this tool. I prefer to take sweeping cuts from the bottom towards the rim. The final thickness will depend on the wood (cedar is light, so it doesn't have to be so thin), the shape (deeper is more difficult) and if I want to push my luck. I have made forms like this with wall thicknesses from 10mm to 1mm, depending on whether it is for a competition, or for more robust use. Unlike some turners, I usually don't sand inside. I like the feel of a slightly ribbed inner wall, as long as the ribbing is fine and uniform.

I remove my spigot with an arbor mounted in the headstock, starting out with 60 grit abrasive, which gets rid of the spigot in about a tenth of the time it takes to remount and turn it off. I then sand the base down to the finer grits, usually reusing the sandpaper I used for the outside sanding.

Where Stephen Hughes forsook a natural edge on his hollow form, because of borer tracks in the wood, I took the opposite view. The rim of my piece had been tunnelled by lictus borers. I quite like the patterns left by borers, so when the piece was finished I used my Proxxon minidrill to clean out the holes and emphasise then. In fact, I was a bit unhappy with the balance of the holes, so I aded a few of my own with different-sized drill bits in the Proxxon. Interestingly, I was once told by a competition steward that my natural edge was 'unnatural' because I suppose he thought natural egdges sprang untouched from the tree!

For me, the finished product is interting. The grain patterns seem to cascade down from the natural edge and the rough rim contrasts nicely with the smooth, refined shape of the exterior. I turned eight natural-edged vessels from the same trunk and esperimented with the shapes with varying degrees of success.

In contrasting my work with Stephen's there is no suggestion that one way is better than the other. I am sure Stephen would agree that the differences are what make modern turning such an adventure.

1. Terry Martin refers to Stephen Hughes story on Turning a Hollow Form.

Multi-Axis Salt and Pepper Shakers

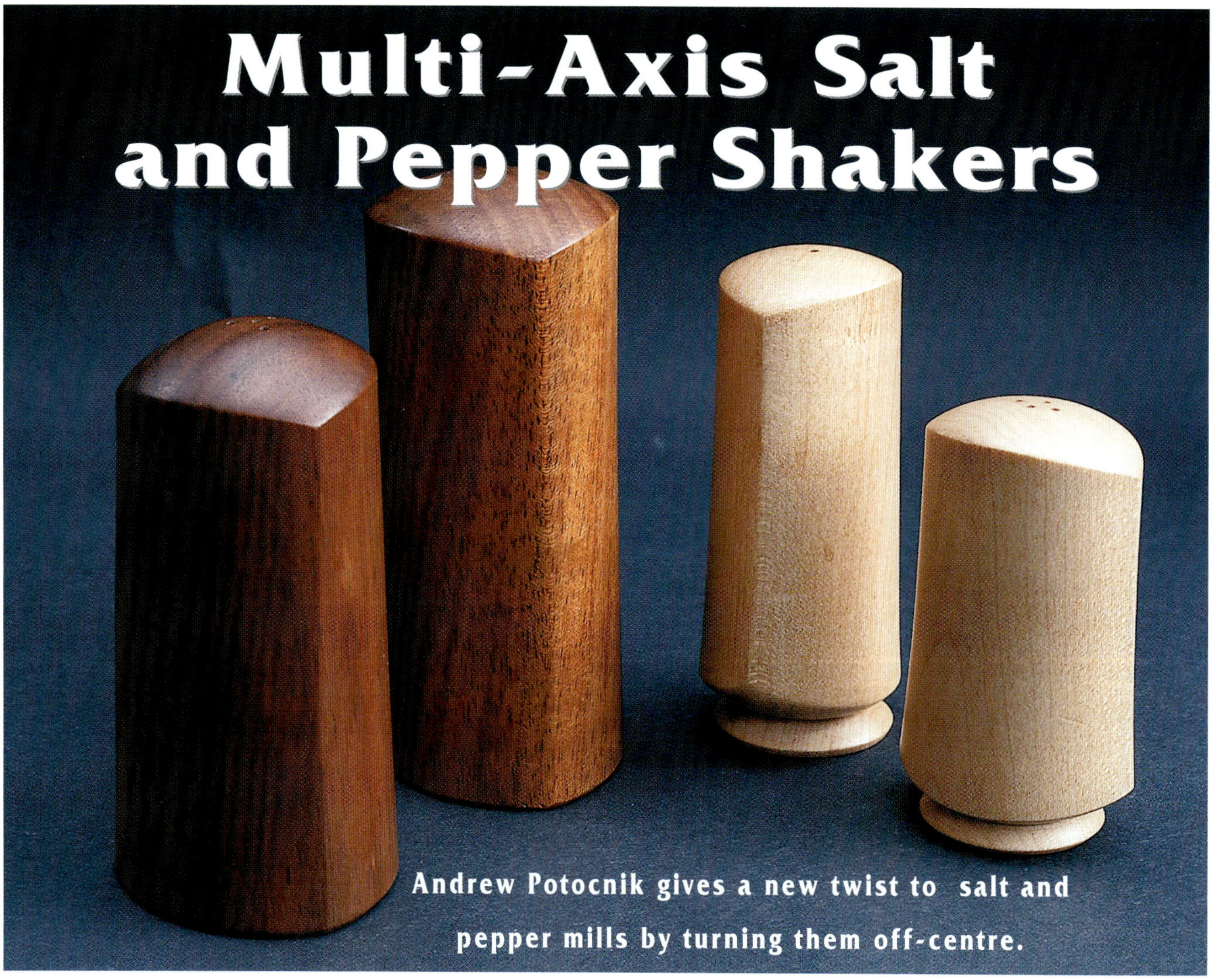

Andrew Potocnik gives a new twist to salt and pepper mills by turning them off-centre.

1

For this variation on an old theme I used an 'orbit' chuck to speed up the production process. The blank was mounted on the screw centre and its centre then relocated by moving the main carrier plate 5mm away. The square blank was trimmed on one face with a small section at the base

sacrificed (photo 1), then moved to its second position simply by twisting the carrier plate about one-third of a rotation.

If turning between centres, the same result could be achieved by relocating timber between the driving spur and live centre. Once turned, I find it easiest to sand each turned face by hand or with a drill-mounted sanding pad. Ensure each facet is not rounded over into the next (photo 2) or you will reduce definition, not to mention the effect you are striving for.

Faces completed, the timber was returned to its true centre so that the top could be finished (photo 3), then parted off with a parting tool sharp enough to reduce the need for sanding later on. The base needs to be undercut so the shaker or mill will sit flat on any surface, while the edges are chamfered to make it comfortable to handle.

The interior was hollowed on a pedestal drill. Each form was rested upside down on a pad of rubber, but it would pay to make a simple jig for support as the drill is inclined to catch. Drill holes into the top for the salt or pepper to escape from (photo 4) and your shakers are almost complete. A stopper of sorts needs to be made or found to block the bottom. You can convert the shakers to mills by fitting a grinding mechanism, but you will need to allow for the extra expense.

Knobs and Handles

Andrew Potocnik comes to grips with the turning of knobs and handles.

Trying to find a balance between 'artistic integrity' and survival inevitably requires a maker of objects to also take on the role of production manufacturer. Perhaps you have developed your own bread and butter lines or you may have bulk orders to fill. I have a number of clients who require a variety of furniture componentry and frequently the request is for knobs or cabinet handles.

Turning something for yourself gives you the luxury of making each item individually, taking as much time as you feel is needed. However, if you are making for someone who is also working to a price, then you need to look at ways of speeding up your production technique and eliminating overlapping procedures in order to reduce time, which equates to money.

Recently I was contacted by a client who needed several turned knobs for the doors and drawers of his custom constructed buffet. His request was for a fairly traditional but nevertheless distinctive shape, which wouldn't protrude too far, but still be easy to grip. Unfortunately for me, what this person had in mind was something very similar to a kitsch, mass-produced radiata pine knob available at any hardware shop. This created a dilemma, should I simply churn out an order, or influence the client's tastes?

After discussing and sketching several possibilities, a design which satisfied both of us was developed. I then produced actual size scale drawings and gained the approval of the client. For some commissions it may be worth producing sample turnings to assist the selection process. These, and examples of past work, may also be useful for showing to future clients.

Keeping records of designs, sizes, materials, production times and other details will not only assist future quotations, but will prove invaluable should

a dispute arise. When quoting you should take into account the time needed for design and installation, as well as outright production.

The Making

Once the design was finalised, the dimensions were transferred to a scrap piece of plywood which acted as a marking guide or template. After the blank had been turned to its correct diameter and checked with vernier calipers, the markings for each knob segment were transferred from the template to the blank (photo 1).

Each segment was turned with its own tenon, which was held in a 3-jaw chuck while the domed end of the knob was completed. The 12mm diameter tenon was cut with a parting tool. Next, I needed to create a simple sweeping curve from the base of the knob to its broadest point just before it reversed to form a dome. Photo 2 shows how a scraper was used to achieve the required curve. If I need to create straight lines in this area, I prefer to use a skew.

After shaping and sanding, segments were separated, ready for re-chucking. Photo 3 shows a series of partly completed components along with those which had already been separated with a saw. Each knob can be separated with a saw and mounted, via its tenon (photo 4) in a chuck enabling the turning of a domed end. The dome or knob end may be shaped with a skew, gouge or scraper, depending on your requirements.

Photo 5 shows the final turned and sanded knob profile which was then separated from its tenon with a parting tool. After applying a threaded fastener to each knob, a finish completed the fabrication of these simple but important items. The back face was later drilled to accept a screw for attaching to the door or drawer. The main photo shows the finished knobs in front of some other design possibilities.

Working to a brief or developing designs to order forces the maker to think in the aesthetic domains of others and yet remain true to his or her own ideals. The designer, artist or craftsperson must strike a balance between the demands of hand, eye and spirit. To satisfy one or two of these needs is an achievement, to balance all three is a lifelong quest.

Turning

The tale of a commission and a cli

The blank is cut slightly oversize then mounted accurately between centres. A small hole is first punched at the centre of the end grain.

Commissions or special orders can be flattering and boost your ego. After all the client likes your work and is prepared to lay out money for it. You might be even more flattered when the client has enough confidence in you to hand over some treasured raw material they've been hoarding for years or which has by some good fortune fallen into their hands. I have never enjoyed the responsibility and strain of using a client's treasured materials. A couple of years ago I underwent protracted negotiations regarding a quantity of twisted and badly split crepe myrtle which the owner wanted transformed into useful objects which could be distributed around her family as mementos of the family home. I soon found I had so much time invested in the preliminaries that I had to continue, but in the end so few objects were purchased that my return was rated in cents per hour. The wood was particularly dull, so the offer to use the rest for my normal production, though thoughtful, did not rescue the situation.

Anyone in business knows there are some jobs you really don't want to do or which are best avoided. They tend to be accompanied by an admonishment that the job is pretty simple and should only take a few minutes, especially for a man/company of your ability. One such for me recently was a commission to make several sets of drumsticks from some rosewood which would be provided along with a sample stick. I was not keen to accept the job because it's years since I've done much spindle work apart from showing hobby turners how to use a skew chisel. All my centre work production lines have been short and curvy with most cuts across the grain.

I was also less than enthusiastic because past experience has repeatedly told me that a client's wood rarely lives up to expectations and is frequently totally unsuited to the job. The wood was Brazilian rosewood with curly and interlocked grain and a lot of surface checking. It did not look ideal for spindles under stress, but would have been excellent for small turned boxes and bowls since the surface splits could be filled and hidden with fine dust and *Superglue*.

umsticks

ring wood—by Richard Raffan

Information regarding the design of drumsticks is difficult to come by. No one seems to question why some are beaded and some not, but I did discover that at least one former professional rock drummer reckoned to break several sticks per concert. However it seems reasonable that a broad face needs to impact the skin rather than a corner which might go through. Pointy ends would not seem to be a problem.

Drumsticks are about 20mm (3/4") diameter and 400mm (16") long. There are always problems turning a long thin cylinder, which is why, traditionally, turners seem to have gone a long way to avoid cylindrical forms. The reason most traditional spindles are a combination of long curves and beads is these enable you to cut across the grain, whereas on a cylinder there are always areas where the cut is against the grain. However the good news is that if the grain does pick out, you can usually sand your way out of trouble. As the softer grain is removed faster than the harder, the cylinder distorts somewhat, but slight distortion would not be a problem here, most likely making the sticks more pleasurable to hold and use.

The interlocked grain of this rosewood wove more or less parallel to the longitudinal faces of the board, but I was concerned about the strength of the blanks, so I tested the first blank by beating the concrete floor of the workshop. Despite the less than straight grain, the wood seemed strong enough.

The steps for turning a cylinder are straightforward enough. The blank is cut slightly oversize then mounted accurately between centres. With a very hard wood such as this rosewood, I punch or drill a small hole at the centre of the endgrain (see opposite). Note how I steady my arm on the tool rest. With this wood, the tail centre penetrated the blank no deeper than the punched hole as excessive tail centre pressure would probably have split the blank. Next, lay out the measurements on the square blank, then make a V-cut with the long point of a skew chisel at each end to define the overall length of the stick. The somewhat vague start of the taper into the beaded end is marked with tape so I have a definite point to work from.

I would normally expect to complete a job of this diameter using a only a 20mm (3/4") skew chisel with the lathe running at about 1800rpm, but the rosewood didn't take to this and several chunks of twisted grain broke free, fortunately in what would be the tapered section behind the beaded end. I resorted to the 25mm (1") half round

Lay out the measurements on the square blank.

A 25mm half round centre work roughing gouge was used when the 20mm skew chisel proved unsuccessful.

The diameter is set about every 40mm along the job, using vernier calipers with rounded jaws and a parting tool.

You may need to support the blank if it flexes.

centre work roughing gouge seen on the previous page, taking the standard peeling cut with the portion of the edge cutting parallel to the lathe axis and the grain.

Once the corners were removed I set a diameter about 1mm (1/32") over my desired finished diameter, reckoning the extra diameter would be removed during sanding. The diameter is set about every 40mm (1-1/2") along the job, using vernier calipers with rounded jaws and a parting tool as in the top photo. Then I use a skew chisel long point down to finish the cylinder on the diameters just set.

The best cut comes from an edge set at about 45° to the oncoming wood. I use the skew chisel long point down so the tool points in the direction I'm cutting as shown above. If you have the tool pointing in the right direction but not cutting easily, chances are you have the tool long point up with the edge near vertical against the wood and butting directly into the endgrain. If you have a smooth but ridged surface, the bevel was not rubbing the wood as the cut proceeded.

If the blank is likely to flex, you'll need to support the job as I do in the photo above. Your hand is there to equalize the pressure exerted by the tool. There should be virtually no tool pressure against the wood, so if your hand gets too hot, you're pushing too hard: let the wood come to the tool. With twisted or interlocked grain move the tool slowly into the wood and along the rest. Of course if you have the wood spinning faster you can move the tool along the rest faster, but with higher speeds comes more whip and the blank whirs around like a stiff skipping rope. If flexing becomes a problem, try lowering the speed rather than increasing it. Easing the tail centre support can also help; if the tail centre is wound in too tightly, you can bow slender blanks.

Where I could cut across the grain on the tapered section and the bead, the smooth and glossy surface barely needed sanding. But on the cylindrical portion of the stick the cut was much less than satisfactory, with the interlocked grain plucked out in many places although to no great depth, and a straight edge revealed a number of small undulations. I keep old 60 grit sanding discs which have done time sanding bowls for these occasions, and use them against a sanding block to reduce the surface to a relatively true cylinder. Undoubtedly a micrometer would soon confirm variations in the diameter, but these are in no way relevant.

After this heavy handed approach, I work through the grits to 320 grit and finally sand with the grain. I applied my standard finish on the lathe by holding a lump of soft beeswax firmly against the spinning wood. The build-up of wax is then melted into the wood and polished by holding soft cloth against the spinning wood. The whole wax/polish routine takes only a few seconds, but take care never to wrap the cloth around your fingers in case the cloth snags on the lathe or the job.

A drumstick is a classic example of turnery best done on an automatic lathe which will complete the job in a few seconds rather than minutes—and they'll all be exactly the same. You can purchase a pair of quality drumsticks for a price at which hand turners cannot possibly compete. However if you are a novice woodturner with a drummer in the family looking for a testing project, a pair of drumsticks will keep you occupied for an hour or so and provide some excellent practice

Cutting Curves

Turned bowls often are not as good as they could be.

Richard Raffan discusses why and offers some solutions.

In any gallery you can watch some pieces sit on the shelf whilst others, almost identical to the casual observer, sell by the dozen. The differences between those which sell and those which don't are often marginal and not easily quantified, but more often than not it is the curves which diminish one bowl in relation to the other. Curves which don't flow smoothly never feel quite right, and additionally this lack of flow leads to physically unbalanced bowls which, when handled, feel somewhat clunky.

When you're dealing with curves, as woodturners always are, it pays to consider the nature of a curve. We know that any line that is not straight is curved, and this seems a glimpse of the obvious, but there is more to a curve than being simply a bent line. A curve is a line that bends evenly without any bumps, dips, kinks or sudden dramatic changes in direction. If you rub your hand along a curve that flows, all you feel is the satisfyingly smooth transition of altering direction as it arcs or spirals, tightens or broadens.

To appreciate fully how good or bad or just-miss your curves can be, it pays to cut a few bowls in half so you can inspect the cross-section. Any deviations in the flow of a curve are glaringly obvious, all too often showing us that we failed to achieve what we thought we had.

For a turner creating a bowl, recognising a smooth curve can be tricky, especially on internal surfaces when you can't see an outline. On a bowl profile a slightly flattened section can be very subtle, but the difference between that and a true curve is enormous when you start handling and comparing the two; then the fullness of the true curve will fill your hand and warm your heart.

As a fine example of 'clunkyness' I can offer no better than the second bowl I ever turned, seen in photo 1 sitting inside one vastly superior bowl made a few years later. The inner curve of the lower bowl sweeps from rim to rim, and the outer curve on the profile sits nicely in relation to it so the physical weight is balanced between the rim and the base. I tend to avoid a uniform wall thickness, especially for thin bowls, because it makes for a dull object with overtones of moulded plywood. By contrast the inner bowl cross-section reveals a series of softened facets. The profile curve isn't too bad (as a curve), but it's set at the wrong angle and makes for a heavy base. This is compounded by the internal line which is really two flattish sections brought together by a curve. The curve across the base is actually a shallow vee. It's a classic example of an early bowl where near-enough-is-good-enough and the turner gratefully finishes the piece having got that far without mishap. Admiring friends and relatives declare it to be a work of art and too many novice turners believe them and never move on, blissfully unaware that their forms and curves could actually be improved.

It's also worth noting that although the walnut was very flash when I completed that bowl, years of use as a salad bowl and exposure to daylight have darkened the timber. Useful though it has been, it was never a work of art, nor latterly the obviously stunning bit of wood it was when first polished. In the end you are always left with the form, with the curves. They'd better be good when the wood no longer carries the piece. The set of curves in photo 2 would have ensured a long and treasured life for those bowls had I not cut them to see why they felt so good.

Although it's easy to find bowls in galleries which would give my early walnut bowl a good run for its money for general awfulness, more commonly we see efforts similar to the lower bowl in photo 3. Here the profile curve flattens halfway down from the rim as it turns towards the base, whilst the internal curve is fine. I regard the inner bowl as being a near perfect combination of curves for such a form. In photo 4, the internal curve decides to take a short cut just down from the rim, thickening the lower section of the bowl wall more than is desirable, concentrating the weight towards the base and rendering the whole form adjectivally wooden (as in stiff, ungainly, or awkward).

Some of these curves are the result of lack of awareness, as with my walnut bowl. Fortunately for me, when I began turning, I was able to discuss form with some well established potters working well in the Japanese tradition, and they helped me no end. My forms soon improved, but achieving what I wanted often wasn't so easy during my early years at the lathe before technical proficiency set it.

As you cut, it helps to move with the tool; then remember that smooth and flowing curves come from smooth and flowing movements. A great aid is to have the tool pointing in the direction you're cutting as shown opposite, so you can steer it in the direction you want to go. Having roughed out your

1

2

3

4

curve with fairly heavy cuts, take a final shearing back-cut using the inner edge of a deep fluted gouge as in photo 5. Don't ever try this with a shallow gouge because it will catch every time—you need the vertical bevel obtainable on the deep fluted tools to support the edge. Ideally you make the final shearing cut in one pass. On a profile you know you'll be starting at the base and you know you'd like to finish at the rim.

All you have to do is take the tool smoothly from one point to the other to achieve a flowing curve. But of course it's rarely as simple as that because it's easy to get the trajectory of your cut just wrong. The typical reaction on realising this, is to instantly alter the direction of the cut, inevitably creating an angle which mars the flow of the curve. If the trajectory takes you out into space, follow that line into space, then go back to begin the cut again near the base and set off taking barely a shaving at first as you proceed on a slightly tighter curve. Chances are you'll go off into the space again, so you repeat the process and develop a smooth curve in a series of cuts. If you set off taking too heavy a cut, the sooner you realise the better because you'll have to adjust your initial design concept or end up with a much smaller bowl.

Getting a smooth curve on a profile should be relatively easy because you can see what's happening on the top horizon, and your hand fits nicely over it. Cutting internal curves is a different matter. The major obstacle to success is usually an unwillingness to risk a passable surface for something better because of the possibility of getting the bowl wall too thin. When there are calipers there's no real excuse for this near-enough-is-good-enough approach. The secret to cutting a smooth internal curve is, as on the profile, to move smoothly and evenly with the tool. You can also run into problems when sanding. It's very easy to let a bump develop at the centre, particularly when hand sanding. Stop the lathe and rotate it by hand as you sand back and forth across the centre. Use much the same technique when power sanding.

On small bowls, say up to 150mm (6") diameter, power sanding with a soft backing pad can do wonders for eliminating small bumps, acting almost like a power plane, but again, watch for the bump developing at centre. On larger bowls, you need to guard against over-sanding in some areas and distorting the curve. Keep the abrasive moving across the curve. Check your curves using a bright light and a short straight edge. The shadow cast by the straight edge will indicate the smoothness of your curve.

One of my more salutory lessons as a woodturner occurred in 1977 in England. I had been asked to take part in 'The Bowl', a World Crafts Council exhibition about to tour Europe. I was dithering over which of three bowls I should submit and had called on a friend whose eye I trusted for a second opinion. Of the three bowls I was considering, one was small and turned in a particularly beautiful cherry burl, but the curve across the base was less than perfect and I knew it; I'd been too lazy to get rid of the hint of a bump at the centre. Like so many woodturners who regularly find themselves in a similar situation I told myself the wood overrode that slight defect and that it looked fine. And indeed it did/does to most people. My friend took one look at this bowl, brushed his finger over the offending bump to check his eye hadn't deceived him, and wrinkled his nose as he put it aside saying I don't think so. I shrank internally knowing that he knew that I knew that I was trying it on, and that I could do better. It was an embarrassing moment, but at least the full realisation dawned on me that if I wanted to maintain my reputation as a maker of fine bowls I should make sure my curves flowed and that I shouldn't rely on the wood to carry a piece, no matter how good or flashy the grain.

Now I admit that when making small bowls in production I don't always quite live up to that high ideal and a few less than satisfactory bowls do slip through to the stock room. They even get sold, but never signed. (A famous Japanese potter is reputed never to have signed his work on the ground that future generations would assign all his bad pots to plagiarists, and all their good ones to him.)

There is no reason why a turned bowl shouldn't survive several generations of use, and given that potential it seems ridiculous not to do as good a job as possible. Unfortunately it's easy to find woodturnings, and particularly bowls, which look fine at first glance, but then don't feel so good when handled. It's a sad fact that although we turners have it within our means to create potential heirlooms, few manage to do so, even in the professional ranks.

Burl Nests

Richard Raffan turns nested bowls from eucalypt (left), myrtle (rear and centre) and musk burl.

Never wishing to pass up the opportunity of quality free wood I eagerly accepted the offer to make what I could from a pair of burl blanks, one musk, the other eucalypt. I was expecting the blanks to be partly seasoned so, as I was about to be overseas teaching for three weeks, I decided to rough turn (or part turn) both so they could season whilst I was away.

I hadn't worked musk for about fifteen years, but recalled it being ideal for green turning. Normally wood is left to season and stabilize before being worked. Green turning involves making a bowl thin knowing that it will distort as it dries. The trick is to align the grain in the blank so that the form distorts as you want. As I cut the blank round on the bandsaw I discovered that the musk was sopping wet and ideal for the sort of distorted forms I enjoy making, and fortunately the grain lay symmetrically in the blank.

The musk blank had a bark defect near the top and a split at the bottom, both of which would vanish if I turned an enclosed form. As things worked out this was irrelevant because when coring out the centre from which I made the two small bowls, an unfortunate twist in the grain direction left the base very thin. I was using a slicing tool from the left (headstock) side and this can be a problem using straight slicers. I have a *McNaughton System* with curved slicers, but couldn't use them from the left on a bowl of this size.

I completed the outer bowl, but the thickness in the base was just over 1mm, which is too thin. It would have made a nice photo and you would never have known, but a gust of wind puffed the bowl off the bench and it broke. (Was this deceit being punished before it occurred?) I finished the two internal bowls immediately and kept them out of all draughts and potential danger. Each was sanded but not sealed or oiled, then put into the microwave oven on full heat for 90 seconds, emerging as you see them in the photo above.

It was then that I recalled the other thing about musk: it likes to split. In this case a chunk in the bottom of the inside of the larger bowl lifted and wouldn't go back again, so I broke it free and filled the gap with dust and cyanoacrylate adhesive (*Superglue*). For this purpose I have some African blackwood dust which has been pulverized to a fine powder in a coffee grinder. I press the powdered dust firmly into the gap, then flood it with thin cyanoacrylate resin. This percolates through the dust and sets almost instantly, hardening in about two seconds. Some woods set off the cyanoacrylate faster than the accelerator and African blackwood is one. Being black, it looks like a burnt knot in many situations, whilst here it merely contrasts with the paler musk and doesn't look out of place. With other dusts, spray the fissure with cyanoacrylate accelerator before packing in the dust, then when the thin resin soaks through, the accelerator ensures an even hardening. Other dusts worth considering are gidgee or myall, or any of the hard dark acacias.

The bases of the wavy musk bowls undulated slightly after the microwave seasoning so they need flattening. You can use a belt sander, but I usually push the upright bowl a couple of times across a sheet of 240 grit placed on a hard flat surface.

The 360mm (14-1/8") diameter eucalypt burl was so light in weight that it had to be bone dry, probably with patches of rot, but this was not discernible under the bark. This was a disappointment, because tight eucalypt burl is one of the very best turning woods when in prime condition. The burl was not particularly symmetrical, with the main lump off to one side. It was definitely unsuitable for a single natural-edged piece, so the choice as I saw it was to make a number of small natural edge bowls, or two larger flat-rimmed and more conventional utilitarian bowls. I opted for the latter, drilled a hole in the centre of the sawn face, and screwed the blank on to a screw chuck.

The wood proved to be not solid enough to grip that screw, or indeed any screw, so the solution was to use a big spur drive with tail centre support and rough the bowl between centres. The initial cut produced a cloud of powdery dry smelling dust, so I knew instantly that the borers had been at work, a fact confirmed when I stopped the lathe. The borers had been right through the sap so I turned all that away leaving a small bead of a foot for remounting the bowl so it could be hollowed. The blank became much smaller than I expected.

Normally I work from the left when saving the inside of a bowl, but in this case, because the tail centre had to stay in place, I gripped it by the foot and used a curved cutter to extract a flattish blank from the centre. The sawn surface was far from flat, so rather than true it (as is normal practice) and lose more depth in the final bowl, I decided to retain the surface as a textured rim.

When I came to finish the roughed forms I intended giving the larger bowl a rounded base. So I could rechuck the bowl in order to complete the base I included the detail on the inside into which to expand the chuck jaws. This line now serves to emphasize the undulating rim with its chainsawn striations.

The rim looked very dull against the rather bland and even textured burl so I charred it to give it more definition. I use a gas torch to char bowls whilst they are on the lathe. It is essential to clear the lathe of all fine dust and shavings and turn off the dust extractor: you don't want a spark to get into the extractor. This wood was so dry it caught fire and I had to damp the flames with the wet cloth I have on hand for that purpose. The rim was blackened before the walls were sanded, so the sanding leaves only the top of the rim black and the undulating edge better defined. I clean away the surplus charcoal on a charred rim with an abrasive impregnated nylon bristle brush mounted in a drill which gets into all the nooks and crannies.

I was lucky enough to be offered another blank to turn. The myrtle burl which arrived is the sort I'd mostly avoid because I'm not over keen on natural edge bowls, especially when the rims are flat with extra bits sticking out. They whirl round like propellers and it's too easy to catch your fingers in the gaps. This piece also had warped so much that it seemed unlikely that the highly figured trunk projecting from either end could be retained, and that in turn could look odd in the final piece which would then have a spiky rim with two flat sections.

However the burl was otherwise pretty well balanced and symmetrical, so I marked out a circle for the hollow and drilled a hole at centre for the screw chuck (photo 1). Initial cuts revealed some spectacular spalting, solid almost

1

2

dry wood and a big bark intrusion. I decided to get rid of the latter since it meant having a hole in the bowl wall and I don't consider bowls with holes anything more than that, and certainly not art with a capital A.

Having established that I might yet retain the trunk, I set about removing the bark intrusion whilst retaining a convex profile in the lower part of the bowl as in photo 2, but clearly I was going to need a concave out-flowing profile to get rid of the bark, so I ended up with the single curve flowing out to the rim seen in photo 3 when the bowl is remounted in a chuck with step jaws for hollowing. The myrtle worked and scraped particularly well and wide tissue thin shavings came from the slightly curved scraper used to finish the profile. To support the bowl whilst I core out the centre with a slicer I use tail centre support, this time getting the sort of clean break I associate with myrtle.

Next I finished turning the rim as far as possible. In this case the warping mentioned earlier prevented me from truing the whole surface. If I removed the dark patch seen just above the end of the rest in photo 5, the other wing of the bowl would have been too thin. Such rough patches have to be sanded smooth later. You can see in photo 5 that initially I retained a sort of bead to frame the inner working space of the bowl, but this seemed too fussy with all the dramatic grain, so when sanding (photo 6) I opted for a less cluttered look. Also, I'm passed that stage we all go through when there's an overwhelming need to impress people with our beading expertise. I know I can do them but didn't think they were needed here.

The angle drill is way the best tool for initial power sanding because you can use it with one hand if need be, but for the finer grits—150 and finer—I use a rotary sander which eliminates most swirl marks. Power sanding is a great aid to maintaining a smooth curve as you sand, especially across the centre where it is all too easy to lose the form. Here I needed to further shape the rim to remove the rough area, distorting the turned surface and lending it a hint of carving.

The smaller myrtle bowls were each completed in two stages. Having turned a groove on the inside, I was able to mount each bowl over a chuck so I could complete the outside with a foot to fit one of my step jaw collets. Once hollowed, sanded and polished they were completed without the need for further chucking.

A Lidded Box

Stephen Hughes talks about designing and turning lidded boxes.

The challenge of turning lidded box forms is one of the most rewarding, however for anyone contemplating orginality and quality in their work, the initial designing stage is the most important part of the process.

Of course the mastery of good turning practice and the high degree of accuracy needed to achieve push fit chucks and perfectly fitting lids is a challenge all of its own. The reward is the finished lidded box form, which should be a delight to the eye and a joy to handle with a lid that fits snugly and integrates perfectly with the base.

So how do we achieve this? I think good design relies on an intimate understanding of line, shape, colour, surface and form along with the function of the piece in which they are combined. To develop this design awareness in your box making, it is good practice to draw several side views of your ideas before you turn them. Begin by sketching profile views to scale or full size on the stock you plan to use so your ideas are proportional to what you can obtain from the timber you have. Most turned boxes will have perfectly concentric top views so I don't generally worry about drawing this view unless I decide to decorate the lids. There are no set rules about how deep the base of the box should be in relation to the lid, but I generally endeavour to make the base at least half the depth of the box.

If you are lacking in ideas for designs look for inspiration in magazines, books or other people's works in craft galleries and museums. I personally find Art Nouveau forms an endless source of inspiration and I am always on the lookout for new ideas for my boxes.

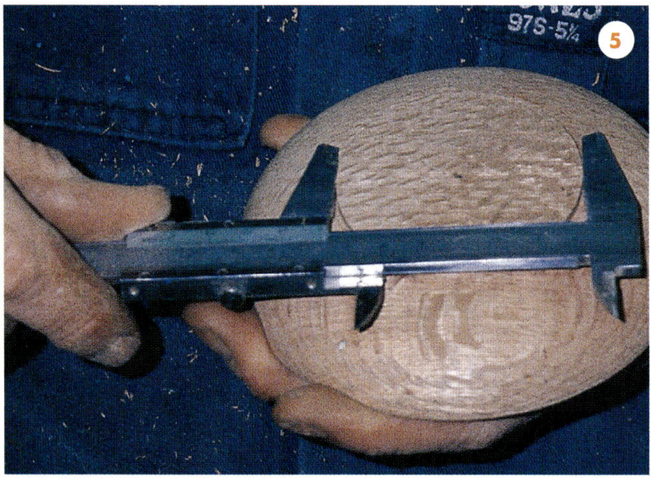

Copying ideas is fine for your own design awareness and skill development however blatant plagiarism of someone else's design for public exhibition will only lead to a bad reputation and possibly a law suit.

Technically your box should have an even wall thickness—not so thick as to make it feel clumsy and not so thin as to render it too delicate to handle. As a general guide, I make boxes around 50-100mm in diameter with a wall thickness somewhere between 3- 8mm, depending on design. Another important consideration is how the lid will be lifted away from the base. A lidded box does not require a handle, but the average person should be able to grip the lid and maybe the base, and their shapes should allow for easy separation of the two parts.

This brings me to the much desired and not so easily obtained 'snug' fit of the lid. In my opinion, nothing is worse than a really sloppy lid—it makes me feel the box was carelessly made. On the other hand, you don't want a lid so tight that opening it makes King Arthur's feat with Excalibur look simple.

To achieve a lid that just seems to glide into or onto the base (depending on how you've designed the joining step), relies on accurate clean tool cuts with minimal sanding, as the latter will tend to lose the perfect lines of the tool cuts. Ideally, you should strive to make the steps on the lid and base cylinders fit perfectly over each other. Well seasoned air-dried or kiln-dried (even better) timber is essential to avoid the disappointment caused by shrinkage in wet timber during or after turning. Green timber can be used for boxes, but should be firstly turned into rough blank forms and then left to air dry, or seasoned in a microwave oven before final turning. Choosing stable timbers will ensure lids stay snug-fitting for the life of the piece. Often, after hollowing the inside of the box, the timber will move as natural stresses are released. Timber shrinks mainly across the grain, so once again choose timber which is stable and dry. If possible, leave turning the perfect fit on the base until after you have finished the inside of the box and it has settled.

A Step-By-Step Lidded Form

1. Unless you can afford to lose some depth off your stock you will need to glue it to a waste block which can be either screwed to a faceplate or mounted in a collet or scroll type chuck.

2. Turn a waste block with a flat face and a concentric edge. The waste block should ideally be between half and one third the width of the stock for the box. This allows you to form the profile of the box. I then turn a small step on the front of the inside block about 3mm deep and wide to allow for easy parting off of the base step.

3. Glue your stock to the waste block using the tail centre to clamp and centre the work. Take care not to push the centre too deeply into the stock, unless some excess is to be removed (photo 1). A small piece of scrap timber between centre and stock will prevent any damage.

4. Turn the profile of the box form with a 90° step spigot on approximately one third the diameter of the box and about 2-3mm deep for provision of push fitting into base for hollowing (photo 2).

5. Decide where the lid and base will be parted. Part a 90° step where lid and base will fit together. This should be proportional to the size of the box—for 75-100mm diameter boxes most of my steps are about 2-3mm deep and wide. Allow extra for parting off of the lid.

6. Part off the lid using a narrow parting tool—leaving the step on the base. I use a power hacksaw blade which was ground into a parting tool and securely attached to a wooden handle. This gives a 1.5mm wide cut (photos 3, 4).

7. Using vernier calipers or a ruler, check the diameter of the spigot on the lid (photo 5). Mark this diameter onto the base for accurate fitting of the spigot (photo 6).

8. Accurately turn a 90° step into the base the size of the spigot on the lid (photo 7).

9. Push fit the lid into the base and hollow the lid out (photo 8).

10. Sand and finish the inside of the lid (photo 9).

11. Carefully prise the lid off and accurately turn a raised step onto the base to match the inside step of lid. Push fit the lid onto the base.

12. Turn the top of lid, removing the spigot completely—or you could make a beaded detail from it. A small bead was turned on the outer rim of the lid of this box as a design feature and to help grip the lid when removing it (photo 10).

13. Sand and finish the top of the lid and remove it.

14. Turn the inside of base, checking the depth before you go too far. The base thickness should be even with that of the outer edges and the lid (here it was 3-4mm).

15. Sand and finish the inside of the base (photo 11).

16. Carefully part off the base from the scrap block.

17. Turn a step into a scrap block to reverse chuck the base so the bottom can be formed and finished.

18. Push fit the base into the scrap block, then turn, sand and finish it (photo 12).

For a final touch I turned fine beads on the base and signed my name between them. On lidded boxes I use either a mixture of thinned down shellac and Danish oil, or a paste wax which combines bees and carnauba waxes.

9

10

11

12

A Lidded Bowl

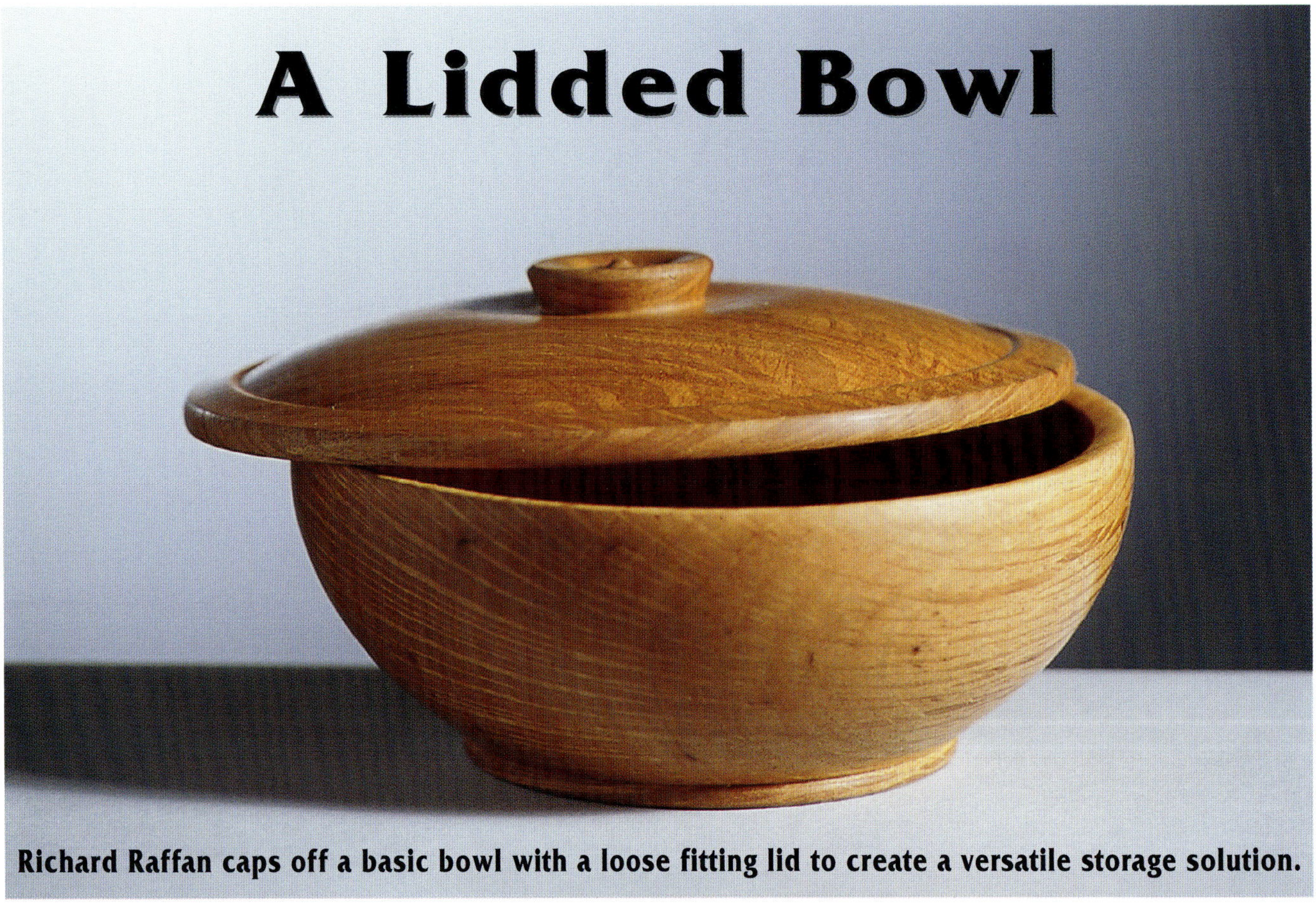

Richard Raffan caps off a basic bowl with a loose fitting lid to create a versatile storage solution.

I don't think you can have enough containers lying around to contain the trivia of daily life—keys, change, stamps, pet rocks or whatever. I tend to use open bowls and the contents get dusty. A lid can solve that problem. It's easier to lift the lid with one hand, so I opt for a loose fitting lid. Also, with the grain running across the piece, there can be problems with warping during humidity fluctuations. Where a suction fit lid would jam on tight, a loose fitting lid should remain removable.

1

2

This is a facework project which uses the two most basic and popular chucking methods of the moment. A modern wood lathe chuck is very handy when a job needs to be mounted and remounted several times, and the chuck can be used to grip onto design details without marking the wood. The bowl is straightforward, having a foot to fit the chuck, whilst the lid is popped in and out of the chuck several times on the way to completion.

To have the grain running through the finished piece, cut the lid from the top of a thick bowl blank. Here I cut 30mm for the lid from a 160mm square of sheoak 100mm thick, marking each section to keep track of the grain alignment, before cutting the blanks round on the bandsaw. Each blank is drilled for a centre screw faceplate on the top face of the bowl blank, and on the inside face of the lid.

Turning the Bowl

1. I rough turn the outside of the bowl using a 13mm shallow gouge, preferring the open flute to a deep fluted tool because the shavings get away faster. With the blank cut pretty well round from the bandsaw, don't waste time truing the blank before developing the form. Turn off the corner and reduce the weight and any vibration as quickly as possible, then flatten the base.

2. Use dividers to make the diameter of the foot (photo 1). If you make this larger than the true circle of the jaws, the collet corners will damage the wood, leaving eight indentations which are hardly decorative. Make the foot slightly smaller, so it contacts only the centre of each collet jaw and the bruised wood is barely seen. Here I mark an 83mm diameter foot to fit the 85mm step in the collet.

3. Use the 13mm shallow gouge to rough the foot to about 2mm over the final diameter—the layout line remains.

4. Then use the nose of the same tool to take a shear cut to create the profile (photo 2). I use the tool near horizontal, pointing in the direction I'm cutting, so that I can steer it in the direction I want. With the shallow gouges, be sure not to use the inside edge with the tool flute up: the unsupported edge will catch. On even the smoothest gouge cut surface there will be tiny ridges as on an old vinyl record, so I use scrapers to smooth the surface further in preparation for sanding.

5. I use a 35mm square-end scraper to barely brush the profile removing tissue thin shavings to leave a glassy surface. I use my homemade spear-end scraper to detail the foot. This wonderful homemade scraper has two edges separated by a 30° angle and 35° bevels. I use the tool tilted on edge for a shear scrape, then flat on

then complete a sweep of the curve into the base using a 40mm rounded scraper whose nose has a slightly tighter curve than the one I'm cutting (photo 5).

8. Sand and finish the inside of the bowl.

Turning the Lid

With the bowl finished you can start on the lid. The idea is to rough the top of the lid, leaving an oversized spigot to fit the collet chuck. Gripping the blank by this spigot you can complete the inside of the lid, being sure to incorporate a bead or shoulder against which you can expand the chuck jaws for completing the top of the lid.

the rest as I round over the foot and detail a sharp angle at the base of the bowl wall. To create a decorative rebate in the base (photo 3), I ease the left corner of the 35mm scraper firmly into the wood. If a sharp corner fails to cut the rebate side cleanly, make an arcing cut using the point of a 9mm gouge as I do on the knob in photo 4.

6. Now finish the profile. I sand down to 320 grit using Hermes cloth-backed abrasive. For the wax finish I hold a lump of beeswax against the revolving wood to build up a layer of wax which I then melt into the wood using a soft cloth (again with the lathe running).

7. With the outside finished, the base section is mounted in my *Vicmarc* chuck ready for hollowing. For this I use a 13mm deep fluted gouge, having my fingers equalise the pressure of the tool against the wood as the base becomes thinner. If my fingers get too hot, I know I'm being too forceful with the tool, confirming that flesh can be useful as a built-in thermostat. The gouges I use for hollowing have bevels of 45° or less, so I can't cut right to centre on any but a very shallow bowl. I find I have more control of the form if I shear cut as far as I can with the tool bevel rubbing,

1. Mount the lid blank on the centre screw faceplate and rough the top of the lid, leaving a shoulder which can be gripped by the collet chuck (photo 6).

2. With the lid remounted in the collet

chuck you can now finish the inside. I use a gouge to hog out the centre, then the 35mm scraper to cut a 2-3mm deep flange 1mm larger than the bowl rim over which it fits (photos 7 and 8). Don't forget that a piece of these dimensions and grain alignment could well warp with changes in humidity. Go for a loose fit lid.

I use the same scraper to finish the inside of the lid, creating a shoulder against which the chuck collets can expand. The chuck will grip better if the shoulder is dovetailed, so I use a 13mm skew chisel flat on the rest as a scraper (photo 9), using the long point to create a dovetail. Then I can flip the tool over the shoulder so it looks less like a fixing for the chuck.

3. Finish the inside of the lid.

4. Photo 10 shows the chuck jaws expanded against the shoulder on the inside of the lid, allowing access to the whole of the top and speedy completion of the project. I complete the broad curves roughed out in stage one of making the lid using my 30mm scraper. I tend to judge the thickness of the lid wall by sound initially, then pop the lid off for a manual check. Tactile qualities are important, since the lid will be handled and it must feel well balanced in the hand. The ability to take the job on and off the chuck so easily highlights the major advantage of this method of fixing the work on the lathe.

5. Next cut the knob, and inset detailing on top (see photo 4). I love to use my shallow gouge ground to a long fingernail point. I bring the point gently into the wood in a series of little arcing cuts, having the tool pivoting on the rest rather than moving forward on it.

Further refinement of the knob is easiest done using the long point jaws of the spear scraper. If you have a range of chuck jaws or the multi-step collets I use, make the knob of a diameter that can be gripped by the chuck so that you can remount the piece should you want to refurbish the finish at a later date.

6. Sand and finish the lid top.

8

9

10

Rough Turning Bowls

Richard Raffan on the quickest way to turn a freshly felled log into finished bowls.

Since I began turning wood in South West England in 1970 I have made thousands of bowls. And because I never cared for the laminated look, each has been turned from solid timber. Among them have been a number of big open bowls with rounded bases, turned from timber which was less than fully seasoned or even green.

These bowls are designed to warp somewhat and can survive in a range of humidities without problems. I make them mostly because I like the concept and organic nature of the forms when they twist slightly. Also they generate a return on my raw material very much sooner than symmetrical bowls designed to remain stable. I love making these rounded forms, and consider some amongst my most successful pieces, but although well received by collectors of ceramics, arty types and others of infinite discernment, they have usually bombed with the wider public (and most woodturners I know) who seem to prefer symmetry and stability in a wooden bowl.

A stable bowl which sits flat is easy enough to achieve if the wood is seasoned, but this takes time. For hardwoods of medium density, I have found the old rule of thumb for air drying wood of a year per inch (25mm) of thickness plus a year about right. A 25mm thick board of Tasmanian blackwood thus takes at least two years to season properly, a 50mm board three years, and so on. Typical salad bowl material needs anywhere from five to seven years to air dry in solid lumps.

Kiln drying is an economically viable option for boards up to 75mm thick, but it's too inefficient and expensive for thicker boards. However, kiln-dried timber is not very pleasant to work, especially when compared to air dried, being very dusty and occasionally chemically treated to boot. The working qualities of air dried timber are infinitely superior to those of kiln-dried, which is always best avoided whenever possible.

As a rule, the longer timber air dries the better it gets, so, if you have the space, it pays to lay down stocks for the years ahead just for the pleasure of working it later. For most bowl turners the time required for air drying is too long and space tends to be a problem anyway: you don't get that many salad bowls to a tonne—maybe sixty or so. But by part turning (or rough turning) your bowls you can reduce the time frame to a few months and do it all in a much smaller space. And there are several other advantages.

When I began woodturning, part turning green timber was not mentioned as an option for any of the jobs we undertook. It was a few years before I discovered that, before the introduction of powered woodworking machinery, no old time woodworker worked any more dry timber than he absolutely had to: as much preparatory work as possible was always done whilst the wood was green and at its easiest to work. Fortunately in the early seventies I could go to any number of timber yards and buy air dried boards of both native and imported timbers up to 100mm or even 150mm thick from which to cut bowl blanks. The waste was immense as I cut my blanks, carefully avoiding the splits and defects, and the task of turning single bowls from large lumps of dry wood was hard and exhausting work (and still is!).

This was my glimpse of the good old days when the piles of thick lumber sat in the yard sheds for at least five years and often much much longer. But three years later the truth began to dawn that such wood could be a diminishing or even vanishing resource when I failed to find any dry boards for a large order—all the local stocks had disappeared into form-work for concrete bridges on the new motorways then being built.

This forced me to rough turn bowls from green timber for kiln drying. It was a disaster, for although the slightly twisted bowls looked fine on the outside, as I skimmed off the surface to true them up, more than half were severely split just below the surface as a result of being dried too fast and case hardening. A similar experiment with another batch of bowls in another kiln yielded a similar result and the exercise cost me far more than I could afford at that time. But I had discovered that green wood is so much easier to work than dry and very much faster, and ever since I have always rough turned my bowls.

The principal of rough turning is that you part turn your bowl from freshly felled timber, set it aside to dry, then, after a few months, remount it on the lathe to be trued up and finished. The bowls will warp somewhat as they dry—how much depends on the species of timber, how much is cut and when. But they rarely split and I reckon my losses due to splitting are less than 5%.

You can also make good use of relatively small trees by turning the wood before the log starts to split. The moment a tree is felled it starts to dry, shrinking in diameter, thereby setting up the stresses which cause logs to split in from the rim and on the end-grain. So the sooner you can turn a log into rough bowls the more you are likely to get out of it.

To convert a small log to bowl blanks, cut the log in lengths equal to the diameter and split them along the pith, eliminating splits in the saw cut. The easiest way to do this is on a band-saw, standing the log on end for cutting what are in effect mini-boards. A small tree—say 300mm diameter—should yield bowls about 20-30mm less in diameter. Similarly dimensioned defect free seasoned wood would likely come from a tree nearly twice the diameter. All this was well known to the pre-electronic age turners.

In addition to using smaller trees than we generally do, old-time bowl turners made nests of bowls on their pole and treadle lathes, creating several bowls from the one block of wood. Waste was minimal as they worked timbers known for their stability and ease of working. By turning the wood when freshly felled and at its easiest to work, they made best use of hard-won material, not wishing to waste logs felled with an axe and laboriously carted out of the forest. It was the advent of chainsaws, tractors, bandsaws and motorised lathes which ensured the demise of all the old techniques, although many have been very recently rediscovered and revamped.

These days rough turning and nesting is once again standard practice for professional bowl turners who appreciate not waiting years for heavy section lumber to air dry whist avoiding the tedious strenuousness of always working dry wood. Rough turned bowls warp partly because the wood is drying and partly because of the altered stresses which occur because the centre of the block is gone. It is best to avoid any wood well known for warping, like some casuarinas which can move so far that it is impossible to obtain a bowl from the warped form. I have had 230mm diameter casuarina bowls warp to about 300 x 150mm within a week, but fortunately few are this dramatic. To test a wood, turn a small thin bowl—it needn't be finished—and put it in a microwave oven and cook it for one minute on full or until it is too hot to handle. It should come out sizzling and steaming. If it is going to warp it will do so whilst cooking or within a few minutes after. Watch the bowl in the oven, and if you smell burning switch the microwave off immediately.

Most problems occur during drying when the grain is unevenly balanced. If your blanks are of even density, ie all burl, all fiddleback, or all plain and even grain, you should have few problems with distortion during drying—the bowl will go slightly crinkly or slightly oval or both. You can further reduce the amount of movement as drying proceeds by cutting the tree when the sap is at its lowest, typically in autumn or winter. I find small 150-200mm bowls roughed in April are ready for finishing by November the same year, whilst 300-350mm bowls are not really stable for at least a year. Two years is better, unless the wood is particularly stable.

If you cut your blank so that the grain is evenly balanced you will get an even warp and an oval bowl whereas if the tighter growth rings associated

Rough-turned bowls, dated and left to season.

with the centre of a tree are to one side of the blank your roughed bowl will warp to a D which will be difficult to re-chuck or even retrieve a bowl from. Plain wood with a splodge or burr in one area will also distort unevenly as it will around a knot or an area of high figure.

There are two essentials in a rough-turned bowl. First, you will need to turn a foot or short tenon on the base so you can remount the bowl in a chuck for completion. And second, the bowl wall should be of even thickness: aim for about one tenth the bowl diameter, or a shade more if the grain is uneven. A 30mm wall on a 300mm diameter bowl should be about right, but err on the side of caution, going thicker rather than thinner. Variations in wall thickness are best avoided since these can set up stresses which can cause the wall to split as it loses moisture. I usually turn a small shoulder on the inside of the bowl for my *Vicmarc* chuck step-jaw to expand against when I mount the seasoned rough bowl for completion. This allows me to work the whole of the outside unhindered, as you can see in the photo below.

For the first few days of seasoning I leave the roughed bowls in a loose pile, out of the sun but where air can circulate around all the surfaces. Usually I lean some on edge against a wall with others piled on top. Once the surface has dried, I toss them into large boxes in my basement where they sit for as long as possible. I'm thinking years here, not months, so it's a good idea to date each bowl so you know when you roughed it—I mark both the month and year.

A serious bowl turner will have many hundreds of bowls drying at any one time. And whilst you can easily tie up a lot of time and money in stock this way, it should be a good investment and better than money in the bank in the long run. I tend to rough turn around a tonne of timber at a time every few months, then periodically check the progress of each batch, transferring each to a different box, so what was on the bottom gets its turn on top. In this way I keep a check on mildew, borers and developing splits. Splitting bowls are pulled out and turned straight away, the moisture content dictating exactly what kind of bowl I'll make. Moisture is checked with a small meter. I have never found that waxing or painting a bowl's endgrain to prevent it splitting ever did more than delay the inevitable, so all my bowls season in the raw.

Microwave drying has been much vaunted as an efficient method, but I have never found it satisfactory for rough-turned bowls, as it is far too slow and tedious. I have better things to do than watch bits of wood in an oven for hours on end, even if weighing them every so often breaks the monotony. But I do use the microwave oven to season very thin green turned bowls in order to warp them quickly and dramatically to create my wavy bowls.

A groove on the inside of a rough-turned bowl enables you to locate it easily over the chuck jaws.

Bowl Saving and Nesting Systems

During the 70s a few individuals tried unsuccessfully to adapt the old pole and treadle lathe techniques of turning a number of bowls from one blank for use on our modern electrically driven machines, but we had to wait until the late 80s for a really efficient modern system when the *Stewart System Slicer* hit the market and was widely adopted. In more recent years other manufacturers have developed curved slicers which enable turners to save two or more rounded bowls from within the main bowl, offering a huge reduction in waste. For a professional, the sale of one internal bowl will usually more than cover the cost of the blank.

If you are entirely new to bowl turning you will doubtless be itching to complete a few to impress your family and friends. Finish one or two as you must, but after that I urge novice turners to rough out a quantity of bowls before returning to finish them. It provides wonderful practice and turning green wood is highly enjoyable to very exhilarating. Thick wide shavings arc from the tool edge to a pile on the floor as the form appears as if by magic. You can get so wet as the sap flies out that you might find full wet weather gear useful if the wood is freshly felled as recommended. But the real bonus will be that when you come to finish the seasoned rough bowls, you'll be able to proceed with a great deal more confidence.

Seasoning does take time, but it's worth the effort, because if your finished bowls can remain stable through changes in climate and humidity, chances are they'll be cherished for decades or even centuries, rather than tossed aside after a few years.

Carved Contrast

A trip to Western Australia provided Andrew Potocnik with numerous samples of interesting timbers to experiment with. A piece of hakea which had cracked after its journey eastward proved a challenge, but a carved rim and stand of sycamore hid the defects and provided a contrast.

The Bowl

A crotch section of hakea, still slightly green, was rough-turned inside and out with a small foot retained for rechucking later. In the short period of time in which it was set aside to dry, several cracks appeared. Some of these were removed in the turning process, however some required special treatment.

In photo 1 you can see the bowl held in a scroll chuck. A step left inside the bowl allows chuck jaws to expand and grip the bowl, while the outside is turned (photo 2). Once the outside had been trued, the bowl was reversed and held by a foot which was later removed. Cracks on the inside of the bowl were filled with cyanoacrylate glue mixed with wood dust. Take care to stand out of the line of fire when the lathe is switched on—centrifugal force will cause the wet glue to spray out.

After the inside was sanded, the bowl was re-chucked onto a jam fit carrier using heat-sensitive glue for extra grip. The foot was removed to leave a rounded base. Cracks were filled and the outer surface sanded (photo 3).

The Rim

A contrasting carved rim of sycamore was fitted to mask imperfections and to highlight the subtle flecks of the quarter-sawn hakea. Again a scrap wood carrier and some hot-melt glue held the wood while a recess which mirrored the outer top edge of the bowl was created. I stopped frequently to check the fit and used a pair of vernier calipers to do the measuring.

1

2

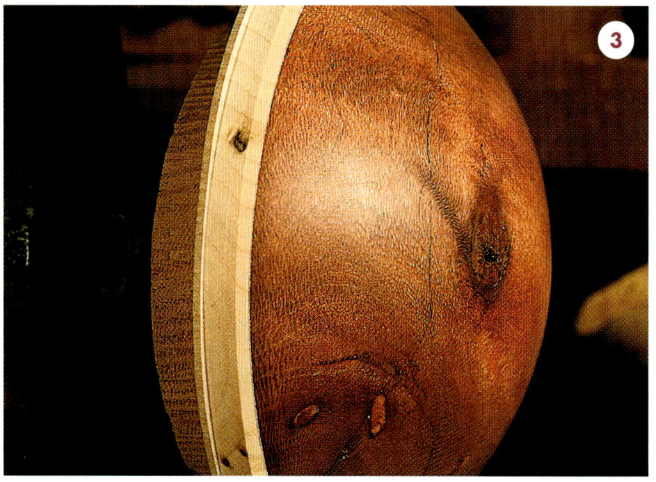

A hole was drilled through the rim which allowed me to check the thickness of the wood and its angle compared to that of the bowl (photo 4). This also allowed a rod to be pushed through the hole to dislodge the rim from the bowl. The hole was later incorporated into the carving (photo 7).

It was important that the rim met the bowl flush, so there would be no unsightly gaps or shadows. The two had to appear as a unit, not individual components. The edges of the rim were rounded to form beads running neatly from bottom to top, however only part of this could be done before the ring was sanded, parted off, reversed and remounted ready for detailing of the top section. Photo 5 shows the parted-off ring mounted to another jam fit carrier ready for final turning. At this point I noticed the ring had distorted a little, so the new carrier also served to flatten it out and let it run true. Leaving a recess behind the ring enabled easy access and visibility, to ensure the bead ran smoothly around the inner and outer rims.

Next came the task of trimming the face, completing beads, cutting some detail lines and sanding remaining sections. Beads were left raised in order to 'frame' the carving between them. Photo 6 shows the sanded ring test-fitted to the bowl ready for carving.

The Carving

A *Dremel* fitted with a dentist's burr was used to carve the rim. Minimal pressure had to be used on the rapidly thinning wood to avoid any breakage. The carved pattern was applied between the beads, enabling them to form

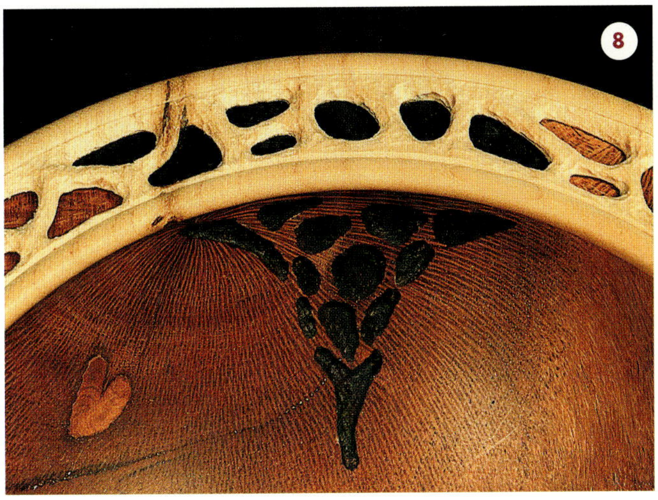

8

9

a frame and a lacey pattern slowly developed (photo 7). Using this kind of tool for long periods can be hard on the hand, so don't expect to rush through it. As the pattern develops the wood becomes increasingly more fragile so lots of patience and care is needed. After another test-fit I decided to stain the part of the bowl which showed through the carved sycamore (photo 8). This provided even more of a contrast and disguised an imperfection in the hakea.

10

The Stand

Wood left over from the rim was used to form a base for the bowl. Again scrap wood and hot-melt glue were used to attach the wood to the faceplate. The top was shaped to match the curve of the bowl using a profile gauge as a guide (photo 9).

The base was turned to a size and form I thought pleasing to the eye. Convention dictates that bases should be around a third of a bowl's diameter, however I find smaller bases are often easier on the eye, so I judge by sight.

The stock was trimmed and a small bead was formed at the base ready to be reversed and hollowed. At this point I decided to turn the base into a ring and carve it to match the rim. Photo 10 shows the base hollowed before reversing—note the bead at its base. Its wall thickness was reduced to between 2.5-3mm, ready for carving with the *Dremel*. Photo 11 shows the base attached to the bowl before completion.

11

The Finish

A polyurethane finish was wiped on and off. I like this simple method as it prevents any build-up and highlights the surface texture. The fragile rim had to be handled carefully and was rested on a flat board of MDF for support.

Once completed, polished, assembled and signed, the piece was ready for personal evaluation. In retrospect, I would opt for less texturing and attempt to refine the carvings. A more delicate 'lace' pattern with a specific theme may have worked better, however it's hindsight which affords us the luxury of refining our future efforts.

Making The Most

Given a beautiful but flawed piece of gidgee to turn, Richard Raffan set about getting the most he could out of it.

There was never any question of my refusing a lump of gidgee to play with, it being one of my favourite timbers and difficult to come by. The half log I received was a shade disappointing. Whoever sawed it failed to cut along the line of a major split through the pith (see photo 1), thereby wasting a fair slab of material. Another split had developed at the unsealed end, while at the sealed end there was virutally no end checking. Some timber-getters don't seem to know how to handle such logs, and there seems to be a perception that splits and defects add character, especially for woodturners—they don't for me.

The log was 400 x 200mm (16 x 8"), and my moisture meter indicated 27-30% moisture. The spray as I turned it confirmed this. Free of defects, this could have yielded two 200mm (8") diameter bowls about 100mm (4") deep. I didn't feel bark rimmed bowls would be an option because of the shape of the log and the grain alignment. With the split I was only ever going to get one large bowl, so instead of lopping 65mm (2.5") off the end I took a bit more, aiming to cut out some 80mm (3.2") diameter bowl blanks. Initially I stood the block on end in order to cut away the defects, leaving me with a wedge (photo 2) and a half round.

1

2

3

4

5

6

8

The Wedge

I squared up the thick end by cutting off a slice of bark and sapwood. The length of the offcut was used to gauge a square (photo 3), before standing the wedge on edge to square up the blank (photo 4) by cutting a face parallel to the one against the saw table in photo 2. The thin end of the wedge was cut into squared lengths as for small centrework projects like scoops, light pulls, needle cases or lace bobbins.

The Half Round

I suspected there might be some hidden splits still in the endgrain, so I remove a thin slither (photo 5). Bending such a slither will often reveal tiny splits, so this has become a routine practice for me. I mark the splits then break the off-cut so I can outline the splits on the rest of the half round (photo 6). With the splits cut away I'm left with three wedges (photo 8) which are converted into squared blanks.

I continue to convert the remainder of the log in the same way, first cutting out any splits, before marking out only one reasonably sized bowl 170mm (6.75") diameter. And even this has a potential defect which I decide not to cut out because there might be some interesting grain patterns and colour. In this situation I tend to rely on superglue to get me out of trouble.

The other end of the log yielded two small bowl blanks and the whole log a few squares and ten basic bowl blanks (photo 7), which I rough turned for a brief seasoning before finishing them. Ideally this half log would have been cut in multiples of its diameter, plus a bit to allow for degrade at either end. A 200mm (8") diameter log destined for bowls should be cut into 460mm (18") or 700mm (27.5") lengths and sealed at either end.

The dense fine-grained hardwoods, particularly the acacias, are wonderful timbers to work, provided you have the tools for the job and good edges. Although they generally work well and can be scraped to a particularly fine surface, catches can be fearsome and consequently these woods are not overly recommended for the novice.

This gidgee was no exception: tough, but rewarding, with a few areas of picked-out grain soon yielding to abrasives. From the centre of the big bowl I saved two smaller ones which I roughed out and left overnight—usually I would leave them at least six months to ensure stability, but time was of the essence and since gidgee is generally pretty stable I felt I would not object to a slight twist developing in a finished bowl. And if the base fails to stay flat I can easily flatten it.

I lost the bark rimmed bowl which developed a crack just below the rim, probably from heat generated during power sanding. I had a few problems with the resin oozing from the endgrain during sanding and waxing. I assume the heat generated during sanding forced the resin out, but the rough patches were soon sanded smooth with a fine *Scotchbrite* pad. The wood finishes to a surface which flashes like a cats-eye as the light catches it from different angles.

About the Authors

Richard Raffan

For 30 years Richard Raffan has been a renowned turner of bowls and boxes with finely fitted lids. He is a professional woodturner and author of the woodturning classics *Turning Wood*, *Turned Bowl Design* and *Turning Boxes*, and now *Turning Bowls*. These books, together with *Turning Projects* and his numerous articles, reviews, and videos, have been a major influence on woodturners worldwide. Richard is based in Canberra, ACT.

Andrew Potocnik

After twenty or so years at the lathe and twelve years teaching woodwork and industrial arts, Andrew Potocnik continues to find himself inspired by wood. In particular he gains enjoyment from seeing how people from other cultures explore the beauty of wood and how they integrate it into their lives. Andrew's work is highly innovative and is represented in numerous public and private collections in the USA and Australia. He lives in Melbourne, Victoria.

Stephen Hughes

Stephen Hughes is internationally recognized as one of Australia's most talented and innovative woodturners. He has been teaching and practising as an artist and wood craftsman for the last 22 years. During this time he has demonstrated his skills throughout Australia, New Zealand and the USA. His work is held in many public and private collections around the world. He has continued to combine other skills with his woodturning including fretwork, inlays, painting and carving. Recently he has been creating large wall sculptures with turnings as large as 1800 millimetres in diameter. He lives in Melbourne, Victoria.

Vaughn Richmond

Vaughn Richmond lives in Warwick, Western Australia and is one of Australia's leading contemporary woodturners. In the early 1980s he experimented with the turned shapes and forms which have come to typify his unique style. His work is characterised by delicate hand carved details and the inclusion of other materials including gold, brass, copper, leather and acrylics. Vaughn has conducted workshops and demonstrations of woodturning throughout Australia. He has participated in numerous international exhibitions and his work is represented in both private and public collections of fine woodwork throughout the world.